Hearthbeat

Hearthbeat

Family and Hometown

Edited by Don Gutteridge

First Edition

Hidden Brook Press
www.HiddenBrookPress.com
writers@HiddenBrookPress.com

Copyright © 2020 Hidden Brook Press
Copyright © 2020 Authors

All rights for poems revert to the author. All rights for book, layout and design remain with Hidden Brook Press. No part of this book may be reproduced except by a reviewer who may quote brief passages in a review. The use of any part of this publication reproduced, transmitted in any form or by any means, electronic, mechanical, photocopied, recorded or otherwise stored in a retrieval system without prior written consent of the publisher is an infringement of the copyright law.

Hearthbeat: Poems of Family and Hometown

Edited by Don Gutteridge

Cover Design – Richard M. Grove
Cover Photograph – Richard M. Grove
Layout and Design – Richard M. Grove

Typeset in Garamond
Printed and bound in USA
Distributed in USA by Ingram,
    in Canada by Hidden Brook Distribution

Library and Archives Canada Cataloguing in Publication

Title: Hearthbeat : family and hometown / edited by Don Gutteridge.
Names: Gutteridge, Don, 1937- editor.
Description: Poems.
Identifiers: Canadiana (print) 20200387189
    | Canadiana (ebook) 20200392581
    | ISBN 9781989786222 (softcover)
    | ISBN 9781989786239 (ebook)
Subjects: LCSH: Families—Poetry.
    | LCSH: Home—Poetry.
    | LCSH: Poetry, Modern—21st century.
Classification: LCC PN6110.F32 H43 2020
    | DDC 808.81/93525—dc23

To the core called family.

Table of Contents

(*Authors listed by alphabetical order by last name*)

– Lee Beavington – *p. 109*
– Sharon Berg – *p. 121*
– Ariane Blackman – *p. 125*
– William Bonnell – *p. 56*
– Ronnie R. Brown – *p. 18*
– April Bulmer – *p. 70*
– Lidia Chiarelli – *p. 28*
– Robert Currie – *p. 47*
– Chip Dameron – *p. 11*
– James Deahl – *p. 9*
– Bernadette Gabay Dyer – *p. 5*
– Daniela Elza – *p. 24*
– Lesley-Anne Evans – *p. 34*
– Kate Marshall Flaherty – *p. 94*
– Roy Geiger – *p. 90*
– Katherine L. Gordon – *p. 130*
– Elizabeth Greene – *p. 112*
– Andreas Gripp – *p. 99*
– Richard M. Grove – *p 127*
– Richard Harrison – *p. 115*
– Farideh Hassanzadeh – *p. 7*
– Rhoda Hassmann – *p. 73*
– Laurence Hutchman – *p. 81*
– Keith Inman – *p. 10*
– Debbie Okun Hill – *p. 98*
– Ellen S. Jaffe – *p. 114*
– Betsy Joseph – *p. 23*
– Paul Kelley – *p. 67*
– Glenn Kletke – *p. 118*
– Ruth Latta – *p. 12*
– Donna Langevin – *p. 20*
– John B. Lee – *p. 1*
– John Di Leonardo – *p. 13*

– Lisa Makarchuk – *p. 33*
– David Malone – *p. 41*
– Blaine Marchand – *p. 64*
– Callista Markotich – *p. 87*
– Elizabeth McCallister – *p. 51*
– Susan McMaster – *p. 103*
– Roger Nash – *p. 106*
– Chris Pannell – *p. 63*
– David Pratt – *p. 66*
– Sally Quon – *p. 69*
– Kathy Robertson – *p. 74*
– Peggy Roffey – *p. 124*
– Linda Rogers – *p. 61*
– Basudhara Roy – *p. 44*
– Guy Simser – *p. 119*
– K.V. Skene – *p. 84*
– Nathalie Sorensen – *p. 92*
– Glen Sorestad – *p. 132*
– Dawn Steiner – *p. 107*
– Brian T. W. Way – *p. 79*
– Max Vandersteen – *p. 77*
– Wendy Visser – *p. 54*
– Elana Wolff – *p. 39*
– Jan Wood – *p. 93*
– Anna Yin – *p. 30*

Poems From the Editor – *p. 135*
A Short Bio for the Editor – *p. 147*
An Essay on *Hearthbeat* by M.Sc. Miguel Ángel Olivé Iglesias – *p. 149*
Author Bios – *p. 161*

John B. Lee

After the Bath

after the bath
on the summer farmhouse lawn
to the south of the house
the blue-white water remains
in the soapy
Archimedes of the galvanized
tub that once upon a time
contained
the naked eureka
of the day-soiled boy
and that grey O
sloshed with both
the dipping *in* and
the leaping *out*
of a minnow's worth
of what was *me*
clean to the heart
and shining
to the very nails
schooled by the sudsy
sting and briefly blurry
glycerin of the slippery bar
that shot from my squeeze
and leapt in an rainbow arc
over the tin rim and into the softening green
as though I were
tossing a fish to the shore
from a river
I'd trapped in a bowl

and I stood in the shiver
with grass blades lashing my toes
like the threads of a gown
as my mother
came gripping a towel
a flag of love
she meant for the nation of me
and I newly cloaked like a terrycloth king
a hero of saltwater stripes
ran quickly away from my youth
in primordial mornings kept close to the heel
by the shade

Into the Red Mist
Frank Emerick—First Lincoln Militia (1791-1881)

walking through the smoulder of sorrow
into the red mist
of an unfinished war
into the cordite-fragrant
crimson burn of old summer
from the musket volley
of a violent Niagara night
that fatal flash
of a flaming enfilade
what carried death
to the throat of evening
death to the breath
with a worm in the wool
where it stops the heart
like the deep brand
of a closing over wounded o
an ingot cracking the rib
and searing the lung
of a no-longer standing man

what also blasts the snow
and breaks the ice
in the ghost march
of a cold hour
where the land lies
blue shadowed
and clay breasted
with frozen-over forms
of shocked-as-they-fall corpses
braving the unbreachable darkness
like the upheaved shapes of shallow graves

he of the lowest rank
a common fellow
caught up
in the accident of health and youth

at a bellum hour
in the age of mars
among farmers
and all the other one-cow neighbours
and hardscrabble strangers
of a map too young to know
he on the Lincoln flank
who learned at Lundy's Lane
and then in the frost-ache of winter
at Ogdensburg
and again at Crysler's farm
how quick
as a sewn meadow
the scatter-loss of the broadcast seed
of a single season
might green the names
of a dozen anonymous men
then moss the stones
to blacken the marks
of unreadable worth
where only the lichen lives

he   my ancestor
he   my grandfather thrice removed
survived the conflagration
survived his lost son John
lived on in the shelter of peace
a nonagenarian sire
a free man, Francis
American born
walking the trace lines
of heavy horses
in this foreign field
with gull hunger
worming his wake
under weather of heaven
God-shouldered with rain

Bernadette Gabay Dyer

Edmund – Our Father

As a child you looked into the face of the sea
Where waves coiled and lashed
Against the eye of the salty North Coast wind,
And Edmund, what did you see?
How far did your thoughts fly?
We wonder,
Did you ever think of me?
We your future children
Left lonely and wandering.

Were we first molded in sand and sweat,
With the scent of the sea,
And with hair that duplicated the flow,
The sway, the rhythm of the dancing waves
Awash with weeds that flaunted
Upon the face of that sea?
And were our eyes ever as green as yours,
Or as pale as the distant horizon
That stretched silently
Into your far tomorrows
Beside the beach, where you were born in Montego Bay?

And if I were to frequent that haunt,
That exact location, the very indentation
Where you sat beneath racing clouds,
Your thoughts taking root like trees
In the hot white sand that blows a storm of memories
    yet to be,
I could be there precisely
Where broken boats are strewn
In the blazing sun to become

Wonderous wreckages, as white as bones,
While you gazed and dreamed,
Where something male in the cheek of the beach,
The cut of its jaw, where it touches the reef
Now reminds me of you,
And where its fingers touch the shore,
Is that where you will be?

Farideh Hassanzadeh

Love Song For Love (1)

Our paths cross
as I walk to the kitchen
and you to your desk.
I think of the unwashed dishes.
You think of the undone records.

We pass by each other
without casting a half-look;
only at midnight
may our bodies find a time
to speak to each other.

But, in spite of the harassing silence,
in spite of distressing absence of dreams
I have no doubts that the Earth is keeping
its course only because of you.
And the moment I lose you
the heart of the sun will stop beating.

Love song for love (3)

A house of road dust
Its windows made of spring
and the aroma of wild flowers.

In this bedroom
my little angel is asleep
on the blue wings of her dreams,

In that one, my little cavalier sleeps
with a smile on his face, as white as the teeth
the angels are sowing in his mouth ....

And on the sleepless prayer rug
my husband, speaking with God:
A man who has united into himself
all my broken parts.

In this home
oblivious to months and minutes;
poetry passes the night
to wake up in the morning
with the toys of my children .

James Deahl

Hiorra Summer

Every boyhood summer
we'd visit the old home Ulysses built
on the high slopes of Chestnut Ridge.
When thunder invaded the night
I would listen to the mountains,
try to catch their words
when they thought no one could hear.

August's lightning would come by stealth,
the way death might strike a young man
with a bad heart, he never knowing
how beautiful his last breath could be.
In the night the long-dead miners
were released from their mausoleum
of sulphur and coal, from their dreamless sleep.

Within the storm's aura their lives
were more than lives, their goodness
retained in family legend,
all else cleansed by nature's violence.
This is what the mountains whispered
when darkness came down the ridge
to silence all our clocks.

Keith Inman

Horses Against the Horizon
After Frederick Phillip Grove's 'Settlers of the Marsh'

She kept lifting bales
stacking them
where they hadn't been

waiting for the pain
Nana told her about
after church
that sunny day with frost
nipping her spotted apples.

She thought she might have to re-stack
in this time without a barn raising
and the children thin
and weak with summer soup spooned
into mouths leaned
over wide white bowls

and then another mouth to feed
at the unvarnished table
in a year of too much rain
followed by drought.

It came sharp
like light cracking the sky
as thunder bent her
into wind-whipped wheat

her tongue gripping the roof,
the stench of blood rising
and her man out riding the sun.

Chip Dameron

Mama Buddha

Amid the wrinkled women and sunlit
hothouse blooms she waits in a wheelchair
for a pianist to play old standards,
and I wonder where she is wandering,
Mama Buddha centering my life
as the world tilts toward the forties,
New York nights and wartime love,
the link to the effervescent click
of who and now and yes yes yes,
a young world full of daily terror,
and now I sit and rub her hands
with lotion, kneading them softly
with old words, the touch of skin
to kindred skin all I can hope to heal.

Previously published in "Waiting for an Etcher" Lama UP, 2015

Ruth Latta

Milk

Gentle, with a deer-face
Blossom gave us the staple
of our childhood meals.

Mother bought this Jersey with her last pay
in 1941, when she left teaching
to raise a family.

Blossom was like Mother,
alMilkways there,
scented like sweet clover in green pastures
where poplars whispered in the sun.

Bones turn to flowers
while tears stream like pouring milk.
Mourning has a reason
but no special season.

I never asked my mother
why "Blossom", rather than "Bossy,"
or "Clarabelle?" Never wondered
until it was too late to ask.
Never inquired about many things
both trivial and profound.

Then, in a bargain book bin
my hand touched a classic Mother loved.
Never thought I'd want to read
Glengarry School Days.

At home, turning rag pages
rough as an udder
I read about a Jersey cow named Blossom.

John Di Leonardo

Mother's Day in Marble City
(Inspired by Walter S. Landor's "Grieving Mother"
Tomb Sculpture, 1864. English Cemetery, Florence)

How can she sing with veiled feet
two gold bands on her chain
grass hard with chill

under the cypress bough
meadows offering memories
unplucked as lyres hang, silently

swaying in the marble city
while birds close for the evening
in the far off burning skies

Previously published in, "Conditions of Desire," Hidden Brook Press, 2018

Ciao Ovide

Inspired by E. Ferrante's "Ovidio Nasone" Sculpture, 1887, Sulmona, Italy.

Fifty Years —
I have returned to our hills
beloved poplars, scented rhythms
of pastas and wines, memories

I shall not taste again, departing
at sunrise, half-choked with every breath
lower lip quivering
your bronze eyes growing wide

Previously published in, "Conditions of Desire," Hidden Brook Press, 2018

Divorced Birthday

Inspired by Wayne Thiebaud's "Cake" Oil, 1963.

A simple slice of cake, a cherry
a brother-in-law's birthday
recognizable motifs –

His circular-swank stories
triangular intrigue on beaches
the couch

his crash by four a.m.
most jolly, cacophonous
in apnea rhythms

morning's green gills
sipping black coffee, apologies
for vague memories, shattered glass

Previously published in, "Conditions of Desire," Hidden Brook Press, 2018

As the Steeples Slept

Inspired by an anonymous photograph, Southern Italy, c. 1935-45.

Mama chose not to buy shoes, walks
on stones to bless her little girl

(From the shadows
my sister's smile perfect, a white
first communion)

unaware —
mama's dignity, comfort at being mortal
barefoot, holds Christ's little bride

Years later
a black and white photograph
where the mind wavers waking alone

(in the dark
shuddering, have I loved, have I loved,
have I loved enough?)

Previously published in, "Conditions of Desire," Hidden Brook Press, 2018

Sweetheart

Inspired by E. Manet's, "A Bar at the Folies–Bergère" 1882.

Between storms
your tears like rain,
all colours washed away.

This grey man you married –
will he erase you, muddy
you with love?

I will always wait
by the kitchen window
for your safe return…

I see your fevered flush
around that wine glass
you caress or hold

to prop-up this love
this anonymous fog
who thinks himself genius.

In our bones we all know
sweetheart, real genius
unfurls rainbows in others.

Previously published in, "Conditions of Desire," Hidden Brook Press, 2018

Ronnie R. Brown

Home Again

You pull into that familiar drive
expecting everything to be
the same: crocheted afghan
on the couch, aroma of fresh-baked
cookies in the air, the flowers,
photographs, figurines neatly arranged on the huge
cabinet-style t.v.

And it's all there just as before, just
as you knew it would be.
A perfect picture and then
they come into view.

Shrunken somehow, their skin
like ancient cellophane,
so slow you hold your breath
as they wrench themselves
from the cradle of easy chairs
to welcome you home again.

Awkwardly, you wedge yourself
back into the pattern
of their lives: early mornings, bland
suppers at five, lights
out by eleven-fifteen.

You sit silent
through the hundred tiny nights
 that punctuate their days. One
or the other nodding off,
oblivious to conversation, the blare
of the ever-present television.

More than a decade before
they laughed at the way
you kept watch
over their infant grandchild
as he slept. Now,
when the droop of a head
a sudden muffled snore
announces their sleep you try to look away
but can't.

Embarrassed, yet still
you stare, concentrating
on the shallow rise and fall
 of chest. Praying
as you did so many years before
willing breath to follow breath.

Previously published in, "States of matter", Black Moss Press, 2005

Donna Langevin

Rockathon

May 26, 1930, in my grandmother's voice.

I remember a huge rec room
filled with rocking chairs.
One of them is empty.
Dressed in an ill-fitting *salopette**
I join the fools, madwomen and miserably sane
inmates of Saint Jean de Dieu asylum, taking their place
in a rockathon, the only escape left to us
in this "haven" of locks, keys and chains,
dark cells and night buckets.

Resting my arms on the chair's wooden ones,
my bare feet pushing the floor,
eyes closed, I rock
back and forth, back and forth
until I'm asleep in my cradle.
My parents are swaying,
smiles beaming down on me
in a softly-lit room.

Far from these wards
where nuns reign supreme
and punishments are meted out
by rough guards,
I gallop on my rocking horse
through succulent meadows,
jump over fences, race with a train.
Other escapees rock to our rhythms
our kitchen shakes,

corn-flour soup with lumps big as cockroaches
spills from great cauldrons,
tomato sauce bleeds down the halls
into foundation cracks

My husband and I honeymoon on The *Stella Polaris*,
fox-trotting on deck
to *Hold that Tiger* and *Hello My Baby*,

later, our bodies rock the bed,
waves surging swelling curling cresting
to lift us again and again,

The inmates and I rock so hard
 a tsunami rises
in this seething hell-pool,

but then the iron bell
clangs us back to our cells, dorms or tasks.
The flood of rockers
slows   to   a   ripple,
creaks   to   a   halt.

Merciless rules
ring us back from
our brief prison break.

**Salopette: French for work clothes, coarse cotton
overalls many inmates wore at St. Jean de Dieu asylum.*

Sadie
In my grandmother's voice.

I chop my name
      into syllables,
             re-order the letters
to find words within words —

SAD   DIE   IDE

These pronouncements define me
as if my fate were predicted
by a merciless oracle
cloaked in her own darkness
at the mouth of a cave,
              or perhaps
the crucified God,
worshipped by my Catholic parents,
cast his doomed shadow on me.

SADIE IS SAID to DIE —

My birth-name spells out a death sentence
that could be inscribed on my tombstone

Will I subscribe to what's written
and put an end to my breath,

or will I find AID waiting
inside in my gloomy appellation,
and SIDE with my wish to survive?

Betsy Joseph

Dance Memories

Yesterday afternoon, February dreary,
I danced with my mother's hands
to Glenn Miller's "In the Mood,"
her feet resting on the floor
mine tapping the rhythm she could no longer hear.

Putting my mouth to her ear I asked,
"Remember, Mom? Remember dancing with Dad?
This was one of your favorite songs."

Her eyelids fluttered once, twice,
and in those movements I imagined
my father sweeping her across the floor
of a New York dance club when Big Band was king.
Her dark hair rested against his blond,
and they swirled as if the moment might never end.
It lasted sixty-six years.

"Go dance with Dad again," I murmured.
"He's out there waiting, waiting just for you."
My mother nodded—I think she nodded—
as the last note rose and fell
and her gaze became blank once again.
I then tapped my way through "Chattanooga Choo-Choo,"
this time by myself.

Previously published in, Only So Many Autumns, by Lamar UP in 2019

daniela elza

they could lead me

this is home.   a sweep of   sea.
petunias hang fragrant   from open window sills.

narrow cobbled streets.   (old women gossip.

              (a dog barks.
    (breeze.

in the framed light a ball bounces   between
rough stone   walls
                    in an endless soccer game.
 (((echoes.

child voices   rise through the smell of   home-
baked bread.

            (a donkey brays.

in a solo performance light tiptoes   the gamut of
the possible.
       cleaves into the seams and joints of things.

melts into crows' wings   perched on trellises
heavy with grapes.

we sit under.   ignite   with laughter
erupting from fig-lined courtyards.

              (inhale the wind.

                the solace of vines   spilling over
arched passageways   around the square where

the widow whispers   the evening news where
the mare swishes her tail.   where

pigeons follow   the boy with a fist of bread
crumbling through gap-toothed grins.

and always   the promise of   water
lapping at my feet   if I dare   far enough

always   that place where the shadows   shift
my expectations.

where   these blue stairs—
                they could lead me
                              anywhere.

Inspired by 'Vibrance and Tranquility' acrylic on canvas,
2008 by Vancouver visual artist Sidi Schaffer

words I couldn't fit in my mouth

in my grandmother's kitchen   the seconds
    slipped like grains of rice
        across the checkered tablecloth.

my child fingers   searched for
              chaff   dirt   rocks.
the minutes stretched—   eternities

                    I fell into.

at the end of the day   the hours   gathered
on our plates for dinner.

the only source of water was the well outside—
as cold as the moon.   as deep as
memory—
              a dark hole I still fear
I'll be sucked into   and disappear.

on the stove   water I pulled from the well
comes to a boil.

        the chicken I hugged yesterday
runs around the stump   without a head.
it only took a single swing   of the axe.

it stumbles   from wing   to wing   until
stillness   catches up with it.

dipped in boiling water it nestles in
an apron on my grandmother's lap.

amidst   the shifting dunes of rice
                we pluck   and pluck.

black and white feathers
one by one   as if they are quills
I will write the future with   or

the past   that scatters   like cellar mice
                when we turn on the light.

Lidia Chiarelli

The Enchanted Garden

(remembering Flor 61 Garden in Torino)
Peacocks walked
under the night trees
in the lost moon light
—Lawrence Ferlinghetti

And then there were the lights
that lit
slowly
in the garden of a thousand colours.

They lit
warm, vibrant
on the stones of paths
on the petals of tulips
on the water of fountains
caressed by a gentle breeze.

The lights
switched on for me
as I walked
on the flowered avenues
and subtle fragrances
wrapped me up
in the silence of the night
then the flags
moved by the wind
became
the variegated forms
of an incomplete painting.

Cluster of old memories
that today are recomposing
while I hold tight in my fingers
the last, dried
rose of May

Previously published in, Immagine & Poesia, CCC, New York 2013

Anna Yin

Family Album

They say —
my brother, a black horse, trotting amid dreams,
from countryside to city with myriad invisible hurdles —
my brother, a dreamer of Pegasus.

They sigh —
my sister, a plum tree, digging deep roots for full-loaded fruit —
the harsh weather and poor soil fail her,
my sister, a winter pine closing up.

They state —
my father, a golden lion,
with a kingdom in mind; rolling and roaring —
the darkness descends, with sight lost,
my father, a silent lamb.

They swear —
my mother, a wooden house,
with windows peering through the foggy road.
When too tempted outside,
closing the door and learning to listen —
my mother, a hut for night.

And I, a grey duck, dressing in a foreign skin,
a dandelion clock, flying with a free will,
a sharp scissors, cutting paper shadows,
a water lily, setting out for fantasy.

Previously published in, "Love's Lighthouse" Tawiwan Show We

My Father's Family Tree

It all started from an ink spot,
my father took it as a sprouting bud.
Sucking on his pipe,
he drew his long narrative
on a piece of paper.

I can sense his smile,
as leaves spread their dense fragrance:
always his favourite,
now highlighted by a brush —
son: a high-ranking officer,
daughter: a respectable scholar,
(my father decorated each with details
like my mother's Christmas tree),
then me, the would-be poet.

My father has never known poets,
and, to him, "would-be" is worse than rough bark.
(I can feel his pause)
then, a tinted soft orb beside me:
"engineer abroad" perfectly mirrored.
My father ensured his final touch
to free me from starving.

I roll up this glowing paper,
and place its warmth on my chest —
Someday at harvest,
out from the chrysalis of my heart,
I shall start a new scroll.

Previously published in, "Inhaling the Silence" Mosaic Press 2013

Grandma's Warning

The legends of stars are told again,
but all in a past tense with a rewritten range.

We are just fresh-water fish—
no swim permitted,
trapped in this water tank.
Wings are hanging in dreams
where there are many countries
to traverse—with light.

We do have much to say, all
sealed in bubbles,
gorgeous colours, the higher they rise
the less they weigh, and the easier to burst.
What sinks to the bottom, dark as loaches,
hard as shells, are our lips and teeth—
closed and intact.

Yet never refer to us as thin-finned,
and think of yourselves as solid walls
and straight flagpoles;
when night falls,
we all sway like seaweeds
longing to fly.

Previously published in, "Inhaling the Silence" Moaaiz Press, 2013

Lisa Makarchuk

The Battle of Kursk- July, 1943

at Kursk, I imagine
its roiling, up-heaved earth, disturbed
by thousands of rumbling tanks
thousands of roaring aircraft
the Tigers clashing with T-34s
minefields exploding; everything ablaze
in this one battle.

With endless keening
through the years
I pluck away at memory scars
I empathize with family peers
their pain of loss
I sense their fears
I salute and kneel
before all who fell
in those battlefields
Alarmed I heed
Brecht's long-ago words
"The fascist bitch
is again in heat,"
and I keep weeding
flowers grown from seedlings
on my family's graves.

Lesley-Anne Evans

Departure Lounge

When I greet you at the door, you are already gone. You
hummock late under the duvet—dog watching—we know
your capacity to fledge.

They say I should be happy, free, empty nester, but I am not.
I fill my days with trivia, mend a tear, pull a few weeds,
pick grapes while the starlings complain.

They say this is my second coming, but it is not. I wear a mask
of meaning over my naked face. My womb,
my hips, my poems have misplaced their purpose.

When you come home, I wait like a stray
under the table for crumbs you toss my way.
You leave for a few hours to visit friends.

I fill my time with meditations— how long
your hair has grown, how far away you live, how strong
my body—a live birth each time you go.

Liturgy of Morning
by inspiration of Anne Sexton

There is rebirth
in dull feet placed flat
on the floor in the still dark
of morning.

There is creation in the acrid smell
of newly opened coffee grounds,
the delight of a full pot,
mug hot to my lips, first sips,
brain stem blossom.

There is peace in the presence
of the dog asleep at my feet, my view
of Spring pushing herself
greenly through the dusty glass
of my front window.

There is revelation
in how my fingertips leak
onto the keyboard—
all that wildness—words
and the naming of creatures
I don't recall having seen before,
when I walked
in the cool of the day,
naked and unashamed.

Man and Machine

The man in the hat with a piece of sweet grass between his teeth
walking in the field at dawn, is not who you think he is. He looks
        to the sky,
considers the way clouds rush forward into day, bends to take soil
between thumb and finger, touches his tongue in a gesture
ordinarily associated with intimate knowledge of what will grow
and what will wither. The man is wearing a green trucker hat
with a deer logo leaping gold over white, so you might be thinking
what runs like that must be hooves in the earth, land born.
And it's not that he is without roots, only he's detached himself,
        transplanted
thoughts so many times he'd tell you he's not entirely sure where
        he stands.

The large machine parked on the gravel lane to one side of the
        drive shed,
is not a tractor. It is mute about what is coming, what has transpired.
        Perhaps it is
oblivious to how ancestors cleared, carved, turned dirt over in
        rotations,
harvested, now fallow is extended 'til there's no sense in seeding
        this year.
The machine is yellow, not green, does not run like a Deere, is not
schooled in tilling, harrowing, or threshing. It operates in terms
        of excavations,
pit holes, movements of massed earth this way and that,
        improvement plans.
The machine sits while the man walks, surveys the lay of things,
        lines,
fixed corners, hard edges. He takes his time walking the perimeter,
drops spent grass at his feet, climbs aboard and fires up the future.

When I Lived and Died Under the Backyard Forsythia

When I hid
under the backyard Forsythia
at the place
where two board fences
met and maintained appearances,
I felt I was made of sun.
Bright, wild, untried, I burned
the ground beneath me;
apart, unattainable,
a distant planet
orbited by galaxies
of books. My imagination
was a solar flare
consuming each page,
the horizon's long view,
a blaze of infinity
immeasurable by suburban
site planning standards.
I forgot the sound
of my mother's voice;
I did not answer
to anything as ordinary
as unwashed dishes, tables
that did not set themselves
for dinner. Instead
I became possible,
bumble bee's mid-hover,
laden with beauty, determined
to fly while in the distance
striped fields of ochre and green
showed how

soft topped grasses ran before the wind
and how a passing Massey Ferguson
laid them into rows
like palomino manes,
subdued and bridled
by noon day heat,
offering their wildness as fodder
for ruminations of cattle and poets and
farmers at the Feed and Tack.

Elana Wolff

Portico

The world was big before
we found the dog dead—
flat on the grass. Not
any dog we knew, a
stray, its face in May

day light like the cousins':
soft eraser white. Its stillness
got our tongues. Leah grabbed
a stick; Noam, a stone.
We knew it would have

to be moved, but nobody
touched it. We stood a
long while staring at it,
air the same as sky.
Sunshine loosed the animal's sockets,

drew its eyeballs in, as
if there were a universe
to view on the other
side. Finally, we ran to
tell. The distance to the

door was so much shorter.

China Red

Baluster vase, red
cinnabar lacquer,
blue inside
like swallowed light

            lodged in a dowager's throat.
Resin carcass, brass enhanced with intricate
floral designs, a

          large cartouche.
    15 inches
    raised on a base,
stickered where it's hidden:
Made in the People's
Republic of China
Not, therefore, antique.

My mother recalls they bought the vase at a trade-
show, *for its beauty*. *Also,* she said, *it's not a fake.*
For her it summons love in a second marriage.

For me it conjures Ishiguro's Shanghai—
the International Settlement in his novel
      When We Were Orphans

      Worlds en-
meshed & sundered.

David Malone

The Weathered Doorpost

The tree was an olive,
hundreds of years old
(and so thousands upon thousands of jars of oil),
whose every branch had just been hacked off,
as he stood by it. At least
he'd saved it from being uprooted,
but not so any of the others.
Nearby the village had been razed too.
Barely a wall was left. Even
the tombs had been crushed.

A half-day's work to destroy
what a thousand years had built.

He was elderly, almost blind now,
and I knew him. Or rather I knew
his work, knew it by memory –
poems about the grove: *With these trees/
we worship what flows through the earth;*
poems about a son lost in a former
conflict: *In vain I call forth/
the shadow of my bones;*
poems about his beloved
(lost in that same conflict):
*Waves of holy sound /
shape this flesh I embrace;*
poems about aging alone: *Over this weathered
doorpost/ I hang my blood.*

I didn't approach - with him you
never did - but as I looked I asked:
What does a poet need?
Can one write without a home?
Seeing him stand amidst all that
was left of it I thought no.

It was a desolation — the trees, the village,
the living and the dead;
the home, I thought, where his poems had been born.

And what of me? For I too aspired
to such eminence. But his village
was my village, his slaughtered grove,
his shattered people.
So was my gift in ruins now too?

Or maybe it wasn't like this;
maybe it was otherwise.
Because as I continued to look at him,
the opening lines of one of his
more recent - and most powerful – poems came
    to me again:
I've borne the wound of this exalted life.
But aged now I wish to be healed of it...;
and I thought that this village,
this almost complete destruction,
hadn't been home to him at all;
but rather that other place
he longed to be free of -
that had been his home;

the pain of living in which
he'd made clear
in the poem's anguished final lines:
But forgiveness dwells beyond my reach,
on the farther side of the crying sun.

So it wasn't that my home was
in ruins. It was that these ruins
were my home, if I aspired
to such eminence – these ruins
that told of the wound that was
the enduring of this exalted life.

Basudhara Roy

Banaras I

Returning to an old city long
left behind is like coming
back to children who have
grown through time; unfurled

while one was away; stumbled
upon secrets, developed appetites,
loathings, impulses; nursed avidly
dreams, hurts, wounds, prejudices.

Or it is, perhaps, like returning
in love to a lover long estranged
whose face though changed,
bears yet unerased marks of

a longing once deeply felt, of
assurances given, promises made.
Returning to an old city is
knowing that you had once

a heart that was younger, that
beat differently to time. It is realizing
that meaning shall always exist in
palimpsests, in encounters forgotten,

in love unconfessed. Returning to
your old city is an awakening to loss
never really lost, a restoration to
forms known best amidst hazes,

a surrender to the tender stillness
in the heart of chaos where
though hopes come undone,
odes to pasts may still be sung.

Previously published in, "Dancing the Light: Poems from Australia and India" Cyberwit.net 2020

Un/dolling your House

You within, this house is home
to you. You without, it homes me
with assurances of no less love.

But houses must never have to
take sides. For when they go awry,
turn hostile, where does one go?

Let's consider convenience. This
house you keep. I shall, a little till,
a little thaw my own nook within it.

Unstymied, my mind shall there
read fortunes in tea leaves, words
shall be profuse, scattered, spread.

When you want me, call and I shall
appear, expressions tidied, smile
well-placed, voice washed clean

of reproach. You shall, mollified,
find in me all you have ever desired,
contentment, gaiety, sacrifice,

> love without expectation of receipt,
> not knowing how I await restlessly to
> be in undress, unwalled by home again.

Robert Currie

Back Then

Chill evenings in the fall take me back,
the gang of kids that played hide and seek
in early darkness, kneeling by caragana hedges,
behind garbage cans and garden sheds, rushing
breathlessly for the street light on the corner,
yelling "Home free!" as our hands slapped the pole.
Night after night, we inhaled magic from the air
whether running soundlessly with sneakered feet on fire,
or wrenching carrots from neighbours' gardens,
raiding them with care and predetermined rules,
two carrots each, always from different rows.
Then we fled, our shadows lost in deeper shadows.

In grade eight the bigger kids were gone to high school
and we ruled the nighttime streets, walking arm in arm,
guys and girls together, we were the riders in the sky,
singing songs of the saddle, heading for the last round-up.
If anyone would falter, someone always knew the words,
saw the light, heard the lonesome whistle blow
as we strolled together on the Navajo trail,
the Colorado trail, the old Chisholm trail,
wandered through the Red River Valley,
walked the streets of Laredo, crossed the lone prairie,
under a Texas moon, yet never once left Moose Jaw.

We swore sometimes and acted tough as barbed wire,
swaggered a bit, showing off before the younger kids.
Surging with power, we always sang in harmony
and, fleet as colts, ran nighttime streets and seldom
touched the ground. We were all free to believe
in a day when anything might be, our arms
wrapped around the shoulders of our friends,
we somehow carried each other into a future
where nighttime streets were only pavement
and dusk just meant the end of day.

Where I've Lived Most of My Life

I'm sitting on a bench on Main Street,
wind turning the corner by City Hall,
bringing with it chocolate bar wrappers,
a crushed styrofoam cup, a torn envelope,
crumpled sheets of newspaper, scraps
of our lives tossed on the street.
People hurrying by, their eyes half-shut,
a whirlwind of dust rising around them,
I consider how long I might sit
before someone passes I'll recognize.

I used to delight in trivia games.
What band leader once sang backup
with the Hilltoppers? Billy Vaughn.
Who left his second best bed to his wife
when he died? William Shakespeare.
Who was on base when Bobby Thomson hit
the home run that won the '51 pennant?
Clint Hartung and Whitey Lockman.
With the slats of the bench grown hard
on my butt, a sudden thought blows in
on a swirl of wind: Who trusts memory anyway?

Thirty years I taught in this town.
I knew the name of every girl, every guy
in grade twelve, every last one of them.
When they came to my class, I put them
in a seating plan, warned them I was
watching them, but not to worry,
they hadn't sprouted warts on the nose,
I was matching names with their faces.
And where are those names today?

A woman swings out of the Pita Pit,
hair lifting over her collar. She walks
toward me, high heels rapping,
the start of a smile on her lips.
She looks like someone I may recognize,
but this is the moment the wind
hurls grit in my face. I close my eyes,
hear her footsteps fade and vanish.
Trust memory? At this moment I'm not
even sure why I'm waiting here in the wind?

Elizabeth McCallister

Rituals of Shaving

Watching Grampy in the bathroom,
brush dipping into the mug,
filled with white cream
the straight razor
running across his face.

Or Dad with his Philishave
preparing for an evening out
removing a six o'clock shadow.

But watching you spread
lotion across your face,
disposable razor clearing away
last night's stubble,
I realise it's the scent
that lingers in pillows
after you've gone.

.

And To the Silent Room:

I told you in a letter
I was coming to see you
both of us knowing
it could be the last time

I was trying not to memorize
your face this way
eyes teary with age
uncombed white hair
hands clutching a cane
shoulders folding into a body
shrinking into itself

I wanted to see you
in case it was the last time
to be alone with you

I wanted to hear
your stories one more time
your own Grandpa's funeral
following the horse-drawn hearse
bones of his three wives
exposed in the grave
washing it all down
with beer in the pub

I wanted to memorize
how you used to shrug
say none of this
matters anyway

the clock chimed out quarter hours
too soon
it was time to go

You were shocked when
I said I love you
as I was leaving
the bare sentiment
in the condo hallway

The last time I saw you
I stood over you
lying in rest
my hands over yours

Wendy Visser

Drifting Currents

Adopted siblings reuniting
for the first time,
we are unseasoned sailors
cast adrift in unfamiliar waters.
No chart or compass
to help us navigate
through coves and channels
on our voyage of discovery;
the anchored lines of each
spread across the galley table.
We compare the gathered baggage
to compensate against
lack of knowledge
and closed fist of sealed records.
Dialogues of ifs and onlys
blend our voices
into a harmony of here and now.
Before this moment
proof of male lineage
and the same maternal womb
in the construction of our breath
of little consequence.
A matter of no matter.

But now, my island of illusion
disappears inside
two pair of eyes
so much like my own.
In the triplicate reality
of look-alike faces
and a crooked baby toe
there is the roar of recognition;
a sound so loud
I hear the sea shift
as it redesigns the shore.

Previously published in,
Dr. William Henry Drummond Poetry Contest Anthology 2020

William Bonnell

For Suyin

I watch my daughter's
                         steps
                             with care

In watching
I savour to reminisce
displaced and undisturbed,

I forecast in cautious speculation,
dark in star,
light unhindered,
dreams down green pathways
my barefoot nomad trodding

And all that I,
as distant sentry
of encroaching fears
aching and useless
to forestall or tell
the unkempt and lashing
                     bewilderments to come
I watch my daughter
                     wander

Grandmother

In the photograph
her eyes are bright,
alert.
There is a sense
of the timorous,
perched moment
of a bird.
That is part
of her allure.
The delicate fingertips
of one hand
are poised
on an armrest.
In the other
she holds
a coquette's
paper fan.
And you can almost
hear it now –
the strains
of some old quadrille.
Then a young beau
stepping forward
heart pounding
bending low:
"I would be honoured …"
Almost a century ago.
When I last saw her
she was two thirds
paralyzed.
Unable to speak.
Her skin the pallor
of a plucked hen.

Pushed closer
to her bedside,
I retreated.
But she held onto my hands
And pulled.
Pulled,
with a desperate strength,
as if by some miracle
I had returned –
her dazzled
young beau
to lift her up
up
in that long plume
of a dress
and swirl her,
weightlessly
across the floor.
I was ten years old
and hopelessly
terrified.

Growing Lesson

The tadpole we caught
and put in the glass jar
ate the green gelatine
it was born in.
Once a speck of black egg
with a thousand others,
it began to grow bigger,
a bigger bean with a tail,
small legs just visible
at the back of its pod.
The doctor was polite
and very serious
like the young men
who start out as tellers
in the large banks.
The thing in his hand
Reminded me of an electric shaver.
It had a cord attached
to a miniature screen.
My wife shivered
as he spread
the ice-blue lubricant
on the bulge of her belly.
I sat and watched something like
bird bone limbs
stirring in a yolk,
those bone-white fish
that live in sightless caves,
blind mice
squirming in a nest,
the unlicked litter
found in a closet.

The tadpole grew bigger
and bigger.
My daughter and I decided
to put it back with the others.
Now it squirms along the edge
in the sunlight,
currently safe from what sulks
in the deep end of the pond
and waits on warmer weather.

Linda Rogers

SAY Ommmmmm

Say Ommmmm

You hit the window hard
and your nose cracks. You
were distracted, humming
a tune for your ears only,

something in an upper register,
something written for birds or
bees maybe the sound of fanning
wings cooling the hive, possibly
mating in mid air, but most
definitely not a human sound.

We've forgotten how to do that:
vedic singing, kirtan, shijing, halell,
lifting gamma waves, lifting our chest
voices, making our heads vulnerable.

In other word, the choir.

Now you see you have nothing to
fear but yourself reflected in glass,
so fear of flying alone is your new
normal, top notes sharp as broken
glass. Maybe it's time to think waves,
sea glass eroded by water, now is
the right time to say ommmmm.

The Aperture Cheese

This day it was stills, not a
movie, no one moving : paper
lanterns from China, halibut
cheeks, fruit kabob, and children
in party dresses hiding in tents,
holding their breath, waiting
to jump out, yell surprise, a girl
with a camera, opening and
shutting the aperture, "cheese."

It was labour day, and deep in
the woods an infant demanded,
"Water me, I am just a little hump
in the earth," the last family photo.

Later, she flushed the nickel,
the one wrapped in waxed paper
that could have broken her tooth.

She must hate surprises. So
who baked that cake? Someone
is guilty, not the girl with the
camera, probably the child who
ambushed her in the middle
of a war she'd almost forgotten
along with the names of all the
men and women she'd slept with.

The last time she played the memory
game, she sent comps to every stranger
who might recognize her in the dark.

They all clapped at the end, but not
the child who remembered faces,
knew there had to be more surprises,
more than three acts in a play, and at
least one cadenza that cured cruelty.

Chris Pannell

Father and Son

face each other in the lounge of the long-term care home. No stand-off. No gunslingers. His wheelchair against my cushioned armchair. I have brought his old corgi in hopes he might still be my father's beast, but Quincey points his cool wet nose away, towards the door. My father is a shocking portrait of my future. Having lived a non-smoking, moderate-alcohol, risk-free life longer than eighty years, he now embodies so many medical conditions he's encyclopaedic: a teaching reference, a visual aide for med students, interns, oncologists. He says little and when he speaks he weaves between the stoic and emotional. Steel-eyed. He lists to one side, like a grounded ship – all his cargo slumping off-decks into the bay. And yet there's as much fatherliness in him as ever. In silence and in words he pours his feelings everywhere.

    Catching me unawares, he inquires about my wife and my work. He seems tired of allocating, bequeathing, and approving what his children are doing with his estate. What remains of his liveliness are his questions. When is your new book coming out? *I may not be around to see it.* What kind of bird is that, worrying at the window? Has Quincey been behaving himself? *I've come to realize there is nothing to be afraid of in dying.*

Blaine Marchand

Lunar Caustic: A Studio Portrait
circa 1919, Rice Studios, Montreal

James Rice sang and wove stories
as he fiddled and fussed, arranged
the backdrop, composed the couple,
their clothes. They appear contented
or focused on some middle ground as they
look toward the lens. Your father, age 39,
decommissioned, back from the boredom
of inactive service, the Spanish influenza
ravaging Europe. He's in uniform–
brass maple-leaf pins on the brow
of his cap and collar, three chevrons
on his sleeve, breast pockets bulging,
small right hand on his thigh, left arm
extending along the curve of chair
behind your mother`s back.
It can't be seen because she sits
in a cumbersome fur coat, collar open
to a tousled blouse held fast by a broach.
Her hat extravagant, a pince-nez
bridging her nose, its fine chain
pinned to the brim, two small shells
stitched to the crown, echoing his cap
Thin feathers from the dome crisscross,
arc through the air. She is 29,
your brother and you abandoned in Ottawa,
just as her own mother ran off.
Perhaps Rice, too pre-occupied
with the calculation of exposure,
the optimum shades of grey,

the optical values, fails to notice
the strain between them as he strives
to cast in silver nitrate
an image of permanence.
A hundred years on, the decades
have darkened it, toned down
their profiles written in light.

David Pratt

Underriver in Wartime

The village was called Underriver
in the Weald of Kent forested
with crooked oaks and elms that spread like fans
in the garden carrots and beets chickens and strawberries
cooking apples green as frogs
in the hedges snow-like Queen Anne's lace
you could cut the stems to make a flute
that wouldn't play
a pink baby hedgehog held in the hand
its immature prickles soft as fur
the dimness of the cellar where we spent our nights
when bombing was heavy
my gas mask with a long orange beak like Donald Duck
in the church dark pews and smell of old stone
I noticed the bell ropes with red and blue fluffy pulls
I tugged and tugged and the whole village
thought the Germans had landed
the green of long lawns and great parks
of duckweed on a pond, of the fields of winter wheat
green shading to blue on the horizon
everywhere else is exile.

Paul Kelley

Buttonhole

From one sleeve-flap to another ravelling
up the unowned breeze,
the white cloth of Sunday unfurls,

yellow breaths shelter in the buttercups
in the children's sleeproom,

where they dream
a short avenue of butterflies
stitched through bending weedblades,

the father's edged face,
the mother's scented neck,

the tub of rust in dandelion time:

all that can unhappen,

urgent as brick, as nails,
as this broken paper, this sharded looking-glass —

After the After, dreams
all the blueness
one buttonhole can gather

for half-wild remembering.

for Mary

Nocturne

To say: There were blackbirds in the yard. To recall them. To see the sky with the welter of their wings, blue-black, pounding through it. Wings identical to their shadows. To think: there were two suns in that day, two moons in that night. Each holding the other in its arms. Days coloured Summer again. To think: I could remember this. To know: it could remember me. The smell of the new mother's neck: lilac, smoke, whisp of hair. A hand that cups my head. Laughter thirsting in her throat. I having been. A moment with a beating heart. Wanting little. One looking out anights. Your turn. My turn. Your turn: to sleep.

Sally Quon

On the Farm

The smell of sweet decay
rises from the fallen leaves
and broken poplars
in late September.
Geese cackle noisily,
cowbells ring.
Inside, the smell of apple pies baking,
Uncle Hank's pipe.
There are biscuits on the table,
coffee served in chipped mugs -
real cream and cubes of sugar.

"Gather the eggs, would you dear?"

Previously published in, "The Best Short Verse 2018, Ontario Poetry Society

April Bulmer

Buffalograss

I imagine my father's stone home, a heritage house built in the late 1880s, south of Galt. He tells me, "Just hose it down, it will come up pink in the sun."

He is not well, dons a pair of rubber hip waders and almost drowns in the pond.

Later, we lie in the grass. He wears a white undershirt. It is dirty in places and tight. I see the imprint of moles.

We slip into the cabin at the edge of the water. My childhood is lying here, broken and dirty. Stashed under the sink, in drawers, on the floor. I cough as I leave.

We make our way to the back of the stone home — the old carriage house. He spins a silver dial until it opens. He leads me inside the darkness. We reach some wooden steps to a loft. There's no banister. I lean to the left, lean for my life. But he hits the trapdoor with his head and reaches his hand into sunlight.

We climb the hill where his white Buick waits like a big bird on the grass. We duck into trees. Dodge limbs and insects. I'm wearing his green rubber boots. They feel obscene in my bare feet. I walk backwards and wince. I tell him, "These trees are dead and dangerous." He says, "Nothing's dead here."

But we walk the highway by the river and there's a turtle in the dirt. Its shell is cracked, and the meat is open and red like a mouth. I am weepy. My father looks towards a stretch of green land. "That's buffalograss," he says. It's long and fine as hair. I want to comb my fingers through it. "An endangered species."

Sacraments

Yesterday was my mother's 89th birthday. My Aunt B– and Cousin J– joined us for a celebration at the Country Club. My mother brought along a photograph of herself as a baby. Her fine shaggy hair framed her round face, and her loose gown hung over her plump new body. I, too, was a baby once, born Caesarean section at Toronto General Hospital, drawn from my mother's wound by an obstetrician named Dr. Bean. I was in an incubator for days as a result. My father was at a wedding toasting the bride and groom. My mother dozed in a roomful of pink roses. And so, I imagine myself in the warmth of the glass box like a loaf of bread in an oven. A small birthmark like a stain of Communion wine under my right thumb. Only a nurse lifting me to the light of the room.

Scar Tissue

I am the only child.
A small worry
born of a scar.
Come, Jesus
for you are Lord of wounds.
I am a sad prayer
my father spoke in tongues.
I am a wishbone
my mother broke
in her tired hands.

Rhoda Hassmann

Fifteen

Mom screams at ghosts
wears her bathrobe all day
wanders the halls

police come
carry her out
chair and all

I go to village dances
let the next-door hired man
rest his oily hair
in the crook of my neck

hold for dear life
onto his sweaty palm

Forthcoming in, The Banister, 2020

Kathy Robertson

Homecoming

Florida's oranges
chosen from market
washed and dried
arranged just so
in his favourite bowl
on kitchen table.

She pictures them now
their carroty colouring
dyed to perfection
cheery against
outdoor maples—
bare branched—
camouflaged beneath
sooty snow.

She remembers how,
after their reunion,
he peeled each one
in long, endless swirls
inhaling sweet scent
as it exploded.

How she placed his
ALICE backpack—
as patched and broken
as her son—on his
toy soldier duvet
in boyhood bedroom

while wails
pierced the shower
as he scrubbed
Vietnamese soil
from under
his fingernails.

ALICE: all-purpose lightweight individual carrying equipment

Previously published in, Voices Israel, Vol. 46, 2020.

Just Like Mom

Just like Mom
golden rudbeckias—
transplanted with care
from her garden
into mine—
emerge quietly
without a fuss.

A peaceful presence
radiating her sunny spirit
while breezes
create rhythmic patterns
that waltz in unison
with the universe.

When spring
turns to summer
summer to fall—

winter's advent awaiting—

they'll bow their heads
with gratitude
and return
to the earth.
Just like Mom.

Previously published in, Devour Art & Lit Canada, Summer 2019

Max Vandersteen

From a Son

A fine-spun figure
offering advice well intended,
an encouraging word
or a lapse well defended;

a smile displayed
for the whole world to see
in spite of any slight
to title or integrity;

an almost obstinate will
neither to yield nor to concede
but always a hand outlaid,
through Christ, for those in need;

a sometimes source of wealth
and sometimes questionable knowledge
yet ever a constant provider
of pleasure, love and spoilage;

a vintage model
born to be a mirrored token;
an age old adage
worn but never broken;

a cornucopia of virtues
roled out for me
to swallow and to follow
to live and give justly:

like determination and inspiration,
like ambition and tradition,
like family and loyalty,
like adversity and mercy;

like father, like son.

Brian T. W. Way

pigeon

(my uncle bart talking about his favourite cousin—always known by nickname)

so   pigeon walked into a bar
looking kind of mean   but serene
stepped up where he caught old henrys eye
ill have the usual was all he said
but when henry hesitated he spoke agin
like the ghost of a christmas never bin
its alright old frien
i aint bin seen by noone
and im not up to the old tricks nomore
no bridges or brawls   none of that
and b sides   ill be gone before you know im here
and henry laid the drink down like a pair of jacks
in a hundred-dollar game
just as a woman and i said a woman if you know what i mean
just as a woman sashayed herself one part at a time
over toward pigeon who was leaning on the bar
whats up man
the words rolled from her lips like a barrel goin over the falls
whats up
you lookin for some fun or somethin
ive had both smiled pigeon
and eased the glass to his lips one more time
but ill buy you a drink
cause youre here and so am i
and she put out a hand   each finger had a ring
thanks man   im grace
i know you are said pigeon with a grin
and im an angel who just flew down to this joint
to give my wings a rest
for awhile

on the death of my nephew
(in memory of rob)

high in the mountains
        where there are mountains
a constant wind blows over the rock and snow
        where there is snow
a constant wind
        that stirs in time our time to know
it is a steady breeze like the thrum of a quick shadow
and howls over crag and flake
        scouring them grain by grain
into that emptiness we call sky
it is a cold wind
        a breath beyond the conscious
beyond neurons nebulae and galaxies
a wind invisible to common human sense
        but beaten in the hearts beat
and coursing in the blood that is
        and is no more
all that is left seems lesser than before
        comets diminish in their own light
        memory claws at the night
and still   high in the mountains
        where there are mountains
a constant wind blows over the rock and snow
        where there is snow
and absence   like the constant wind
        absence howls below

Laurence Hutchman

Dream of Origins

I wake up to see the headlines:
science has discovered God.
A scientist has probed and found
particles of radiation,
the origins of the universe rippling
on a distant primordial shore.
I look upon the blue and pink shell—
the genesis of all we know.
This morning in the elegant hotel room
the children, as usual, scramble over the bed.

I am always searching for the beginning:
in the stroller I'm watching the orange sky
suffused through black tangled branches;
in the playhouse I'm looking at the excited eyes
of birds, wondering how I am like them.

I dream of going back to Ireland after the war
to rescue Granny's relics.
Father said, "You should search the photos
to get the whole picture":
playing hockey with potato sack nets with Les,
the mad minister, the puritan boarders,
the old fishermen who returned,
the young soldiers who did not.

You cannot deny them.
You must take your family with you.
We are always looking for that beginning,
that first moment we mouth our names
when we hear voices and know they are us,
when history comes out of the photos.
It is then we cry out against
bruised skin, blind vision.

It is then we travel through the dark morning,
gaze from the edge at the beginning:
in the distant sea of space,
and in the distant, intimate matrix,
the blue and pink celestial shell.

Previously published in, Foreign National, Agawa Books, 1994 Selected Poems, Guernica, Editions, 1994; Swimming Toward the Sun Collected Poems: 1968-2020, Guernica Editions, 2020

Reading the Water

I recollect weekend trips, my father following
red and yellow lines on maps
to obscure places with aboriginal names—
trips that began on forlorn bridges
rivers that suddenly
disappeared into tangled undergrowth,
narrowed to open fields and high grasses.
He had strategies that I could only imagine
as he followed the curves of the river,
a soldier on a subversive campaign,
recalling something, no doubt mother had said,
that drove him away from his family
to these hedge-lined fields
where the water was black and rushing.
He stood in the water, hip waders against
the current and waited
for the speckled, the brown, the rainbow,
moving slowly, until
he chose the right fly, the appropriate angle.
Lassoing the line,
he cast it out into an "s" above the current,
tugging at it
jazzy improvisation
playing the waters with his fingers,
reading its bubbles as notes on some aqua score,
reading the sounds, the currents, the silences,
marks on a rippling dark page.
He waited for the change in tension.
Timing was all. The tug.
He could wait there,
wait there almost
all morning—or so it seemed,
and I followed him, continually onward,
to catch that fish.

Previously published in, Reading the Water, Black Moss Press, 2008
Swimming Toward the Sun: Collected Poems: 1968-2020, Guernica Editions, 2020

K.V. Skene

Your Mouth Remembers the Taste

You know why you return, wish
you could stay. Your mouth remembers
the taste of home, the feel, the gut-wrenching
grab of it. Like a small animal
you circle the room three times, settle,
soothed by its too old, too-familiar
shabbiness. Even if your heart
is ring-fenced
a faded photo, post card, voice on the phone,
the scent of just-baked bread, wet woollen mittens
pulls you back
and all the years apart just fall away.

Previously published in, Reach Poetry, January 2019 (UK)

Back Home

and light from the round window
under the eaves
scans the small space between dusk
and dark and I see

through a tangle of trees – branch
and bud and early birds
back home
to brood and I shout

over and over,
syllables splash into snowmelt,
blackice quick-silvers
underfoot and I smell

greenmoss, watercress,
the first fiddlehead pushing, pushing,
full of itself
as we used to be – not

old and alone and bleeding
like maple – overhead
a grey sky
and the certainty of rain.

Previously published in, Existere, Vol. 25, No.2, Spring 2005

Opening up the Possibility of Perfect

only to ride that memory-go-round
while all our painted horses
gallop into summerhaze, impervious
to the rise and fall of small iridescent voices,
flutter of caps and pony tails, flying high-fives
that cover the thud of hooves
hooked on fairground music; slightly too loud,
too innocent, too beautiful, too
sad – so much of you is part of me
and yet...
and yet
you were dying to be told
what I thought you should never have been told,
swung from urology, oncology, radiology, theology
with a stubborn smile
opening up the possibility of perfect
as sunset, a slivered moon, our sleepy children
all get carried away
to wherever they must go – but it's all right now ...
It's all over.

Previously published in, Reach Poetry. Issue 155, June 2011 (UK)

Callista Markotich

Just the Way of It

Old woman, if you look at your hands lying in your lap, observe
the worst wreckage, your index finger – swollen, twisted, bent

and motionless, yet painful anyway,
and if you remember it straight and strong and true

touching a key on your piano,
feeding the crisp of taffeta

to the tack-tacking needle of your Singer,
directing the gaze of a child

to a cardinal whistling *cheer, cheer, cheer*
from the topmost twig of a shagbark or fir,

and if you recall someone gentle,
your mother, grandmother, aunt,

taking your little hand in hers and naming for you
your five digits, rolling them sweetly in her own,

Tommy Thumb through Toby Tall to Baby Finger,
singing you the song of the finger family,

there in your very own hand, well,
she'll be gone now, of course.

Sorry, old woman, but that's just the way of it,
gone with her reservoir of love and song.

And if you think to allow your ruined finger (Peter, wasn't it?)
his old role in the family – authority, direction – think again.

Don't point.
Someone might think you are casting a hex.

Spadina Story

Jane sets her story on cement slabs
mottled with pox, gummy blobs
fused into filthy sidewalk
studded with litter, covered by sheen of soot,
a rime of cinder on snow crusts curving around
north sides of bus shelters, waste bins, bike racks.
And yet, she says, Spadina Avenue is serene
on this morning, and pearly light suffuses the air;
over there, a restaurant windowbox, smudges of blue
and apricot huddle in a tumble of verdure –
the first pansies of March,
she tells us.

A man bristles out of the filmy mist,
like a transformer, shape-shifting,
popping, hard-edged, staccato
bites of words and phrases audible;
she hears him, he's shouting as he comes.
He's bobbing, weaving, kicking out,
as if harangued, pestered,
on every side tormentors.
He swings and turns, beleaguered, furious.
Who could know what these harassers say to him?
Not she, Jane tells us, and to herself she wonders:
should she cross the street? There's time to cross the street.

No. No, she is a person, he is a person.
As persons, they can share this sidewalk,
and she confirms he is not focused on her
at all; he's into his hecklers,
he's resisting, scolding, giving it back, holding his own.
So they pass, Jane says, on the pocked, double wide sidewalk.
They pass, just two persons on the street,
and she feels the whoosh of motion behind her,
turns, and sees the toe of his well-worn shoe
aiming a kick at her receding backside, Jane says,
as if some invisible cohort has yelled at him:
"Kick that girl in the arse!"
and of all in the frenzy of taunts and dares,
with this, he feels compelled to comply.

But it was weird, Jane says,
how the fury of the moment flamed out;
how he marshalled a mighty kick and missed by inches,
a showy miss;
how she rounded on him, brain prepping lips for a strong
"Fuck off!";
how those words faded to thought, mere thought,
and floated off into the geist
of a Toronto morning.

Roy Geiger

Echo of Home

Late summer and early September Stokely's would be running full tilt, and guys who bummed around the rest of the year doing not much would get on at Stoke's, and I told my mother when I got older I'd work there, too, and she said not likely because I'd be at school. But I was entranced by the tractors, big Case, John Deere, and Massey Fergusons, pulling wagons loaded with bushels of tomatoes in a line snaking up to the Stokely entrance from around in front of the little town Carnegie library then behind the block behind main street that had the back entrances to Kennedy's Furniture and the restaurant. And then I see guys in spattered work clothes emptying those bushels onto the elevator which takes the red mix of pulp and fruit up into the factory. Ah, memory! At least the persistent and visceral recall of tomatoes must be real. The sweet acid smell of the fat ripe ones, the whiff of those left in the field or basket just a little too long but not yet rotted, the dried smears of orange-red flesh and skin and yellow seeds on baskets, wagons, the streets, spillover of a glorious harvest.

Stokely's shut down, and sat idle for many years while the factory's block-long red brick wall loomed over Talbot Street, over the town. I remember the raised landscaping bed that ran along the sidewalk the entire length of the factory, and where, for one year at least, masses of red salvia bloomed heroically. I would walk along the concrete top by this bed, not even able to make the entire length the first try. Beside me as I walked, that red brick wall of the empty factory seemed to go on forever, blank, featureless, and grim.

Big Fish Eat Little Fish: A Marriage

(after Big Fish Eat Little Fish by Pieter Breughel the Elder)

He went to war and returned, but he pretended it had never happened. He pretended he didn't have a prosthesis that fit his face like a nose-and-moustache mask. With strange dignity he sold cars and milked our pity. Once such a promising boy, we had known him as the one through whom we might live our dreams.

I am alone, he whispered near my ear.
Then you should marry me.
Big fish eat little fish, he countered.
I'm vegetarian.
I am one, too, if you love me.
Our child was stillborn. We adopted an agency boy, who later went to jail, then disappeared.

I never asked about the prosthesis, the war, and all that. But time is an ogre to force the truth, and as we stood on the margin of old age trying so very hard not to cross, I begged, Show me, no more pretending.

Tears on his face, a flood I'd never seen, but he removed the prosthesis.

I could see no reason for it, nothing to hide, but by then he had slipped out the door the wicked device back on. I paused at the same door. That night I bought a big salmon and ate the whole thing. I could not help myself.

We have watched and will now examine our dreams.

Nathalie Sorensen

Diminishment

So many mornings waking together,
coffee steaming in sunshine, feeding the baby,
digging garden carrots, reading Derrida,
writing, teaching, building houses,
putting our youngest on the train to his own life.
Talking.

Now our conversation is tattered.
Your ears can't hear the chickadee's two-note call in spring
or what I want to tell you about the smell of fried bananas
my grandfather used to cook me for breakfast,
or even, *I'm hungry, please pass the bread.*
I'm weary of saying everything twice.

In her late eighties, my blind mother said to my deaf father,
We have to be strong.
He wondered, sometimes, if they could.

The season is changing, chickadees are calling.
Let's go around the garden
see what has survived, trim the dead leaves.
Soon it will be warm enough to plant the carrots.

Jan Wood

Frostbitten

earth forms pockets of shelter
under limbs on the ridge
autumn air creaks heavy with spite
something I curl away from
breath is drawn through clenched teeth
I talk to myself in ghostly wisps
as I plastic the cabin windows
bank it in leaves, the lake moans
ice quilts my bones and marrow shivers

December light is devoured soundlessly
the forest disappears in a shroud
born under the ghost of sun
and a jaundiced sky
I am not intimidated by such ambiguity
muscles taut, I arch my body, alert
for shifts of weight heard on the edge of sleep
wait for cracks in the Wolf Moon nights

and they come, the frost loosens its grip
and stares, fight or flight, I muse
if only it were that easy
Snow Moon dreams are anemic
in need of transfusion and full of angst
in my throat is a low growl that warns winter
it has nothing more to ask of me now
nothing more to say

at the first drip of water I am in rut
slashing awkwardly out the door
the swollen willow stems and vibrant sky
are reason enough to weep
geese, branches, roots, everything
alive, reaching for the sun

Kate Marshall Flaherty

For Dad

I'm thinking about humble bees,
their inner instructions to find flower powder,
    while I watch you in the kitchen. Ritual
dishrag tucked into your belt,
you are sorting through pickling spices
with berry-stained fingers;
    shuffling past the sauerkraut crock
then back to pick cloves and crush cinnamon.
    Pumpkin rinds, translucent as honey,
sit in the sun near the sill: bottled autumn.

    Humming an aria
you home in, busy worker bee,
smooth the pricks from small cucumber skins,
nimbly stuff them into mason jars,
measure out vinegar, fresh dill, love.
    Grandma Lucy's unwritten recipe
part of your pattern now.
Pickles like no other, everyone says.
    What is your secret?
What royal jelly makes these
    queens of dill?

The grandkids buzz about,
    bumbling 'til things fly
from holes in the upholstery,
getting golden foam-bits
    all over their hair
like pollen:
    sweet beehive of Poppa's farm.

Birdhouse

on Tony Hoagland's Birdhouse

My dad has ten hummingbird feeders
suspended all over the farm in crabapples, pines,

glass orbs of red sugar-water, some
shaped as strawberries, some teardrops—

the wasps cling to their clear straws, so he put up
tiny mesh traps, to keep his flurried friends safe.

He no longer puts delphinium in the window
after the one mother hit the glass—

if he could, he would make a birdhouse
for these sweet smeary blurs of birds,

he'd weave the web-strands himself,
lift the mouse fur and bits of fluff, milkweed silk

and shimmering dust; if he could, he'd make
a curtain of spun-gold filaments to guard the fairy entrance,

to keep out bees and weather, but make it
gauzy enough to see the pond and grandkids through—

if he could, he'd make safe
the place of mom's diminishings, that hover,

blur her wings of memory, moving in a way we know
but cannot see—he'd make a house to

hold her, suspended and clear as the feeders
shining in the sun.

A Mouse's Prayer

O constant moon,
you illuminate my tracks,
almost imperceptible
atop this thin blanket
of ice-crusted snow.

May you hide my scribblings
and nibbles
in shadowy corners,
and reveal for my shiny eyes
pearls of hard corn, crumbs
and paper boxes of flakes
I can gnaw holiness into.

Send a beam slantwise
into the farm window,
drench the dresser drawer's raggy nest
of tattered flannel
where my babes lie opaque
in woolen scraps;
where my warm lima beans
nestle together dreaming
six-small-parts-into-one
big mouse dream
of nut butters
and flecks of sharp cheddar.

I will scurry my prayer
across the stone mantel
beneath the clock:

My blessings on all cracks
        and cubbyholes,
my thanks for all things small
        and with seeds,
my wish for protection
        from owl eyes and traps,
and things with lids.

O moon, you see me
        when others do not,
you know my brown fur's sheen,
        and you reflect for me
my own great smallness
in your immensely
        dark and speckled sky.

Debbie Okun Hill

When the Grandchildren Leave…

Golden aged under canopy of elm:
two autumn leaves, dry wrinkled skin of plants.
You clasped my right hand and asked me to dance.

Two-step, your attempt did not overwhelm,
sliding, waltzing, this musical romance.
Golden aged under canopy of elm:
two autumn leaves, dry wrinkled skin of plants.

Fun float on sun clouds with you at my helm,
gliding over walkways, all in a trance.
Your crutches, arm held, my love in sweatpants.
Golden aged under canopy of elm:
two autumn leaves, dry wrinkled skin of plants.
You clasped my right hand and asked me to dance

Andreas Gripp

The Language of Sparrows

Our daughter is dead.

We plant seedlings
by her grave in April,
when Spring seduces
with all its promise,
moisten the ground
with a jug of water
and say how, years from now,
a bush will burst and flower,
be home to a family of sparrows,
each knowing the other by name.

I ask you if birds have names,
like *Alice, Brent, Jessica* and *James,*
if mother and father bird
call them in when it rains,
say *settle here in branches*
amid the leaves that keep you dry—
not in English, mind you,
or any other human tongue
but in the language of sparrows;
each trill, each warbling,
a repartee,
a crafted conversation of the minds.

I then notice
that we never see the birds
when it rains,
how they disappear in downpours,
seeking shelter
in something we simply cannot see.

When we're old,
when we come to remember
the loved one whom we've lost,
they'll be shielded in our shrub—
not a short and stunted one,
but a *grand,* blessed growth,
like the one that spoke to Moses,
aflame, uttering
I AM WHO I AM,

one that towers,
dense with green,
a monument
to the child whom we treasured
and to the birds
that she adored,
naming the formerly fallowed, *hallowed,*
sacred, *remove your shoes,*
Spirits and Sparrows dwell
and sibilate secrets
we're unworthy to hear.

Family Photo

It hadn't been seen
in ages
(if a decade
can be deemed
as such),
there, in the frame,
a mother and father
ecstatic,
grateful you've entered
their world;

and you'll feel
the photo
in front of you,
strain a tear
for the parents
that were,

for there's but twice
in your life
where you're loved
so very deeply
(and which you'll have
no recollection):

at the moment of passing
and burial,

and that magnificent morning
of sun,
where you're cradled
in wraps of white,
in your mother's crib of arms,
your enveloping father
proud, beaming,

the wound of words
an egg, untouched
by swim of seed.

Susan McMaster

Somewhere to Go

Father, the sky is gold and glory
as we drive towards your death –
amber swirls, streaks of rose,
charcoal and chrome
piled stern but light
on the darkening grey.

Golden Lake, Killaloe, Madawaska hills.
The sun spears silver and sideways
through the Group of Seven woods
you love, rings a jack pine
in a rainbow of mist
as we hum into the night
to the beat of your
slowing breaths,
last few words.

Combermere, Maynooth, Silent Lake.
Nothing clear for days, then,
I love you, to the daughter
who worries and plans.
There's nothing I need or want,
to me, who tries to fix things.
And tonight the call – *Come now*.

I have one hope left – to reach you
in time to say – *Father, the sky*
was heaped and golden
tonight, for you.

If there is somewhere to go,
this, for you,
waits.

Previously published in, Haunt (Black Moss, 2018).

Ottawa After All

Walking home tonight
along Colonel By Drive,
walking on the grass
and not the paved path
because it's one of those nights,
those Ottawa nights
when the air is full of scent
and soft as a feather pillow,
and indigo glass hangs
where the sky should be –

I think: this is my town.
This is my place.
I know that gather
of crab apple trees,
blossoms still drifting
a few pale petals down,
where first love and I
leaned into the night.
Here's where I turned
my bike each morning
to follow the Canal,
its garden-banked road
that make even rush hour
a bird-full thing,
with sun skip-stepping
over slanted waves.

I know this town. Behind me
the Peace Tower dozes over all,
its gargoyles frowning on guard.
Those stairs lead to the bar
where poets meet to rant.
There's the checkerboard of turns
through the stop-signed Glebe,
the jig past the lagoon
where I skated every winter,
the store no longer there
where I spent hoarded cents
on sweet-sour candies,
the sidewalks that scraped
my bare feet as a child.

Every step I take
deepens another.

Walking home tonight,
jubilation fills me
like summer ice cream.

Previously published in, Haunt (Black Moss, 2018)

Roger Nash

Incoming Tide

"What d'you see, m'boy, when the tide's
comin' in?" That was my uncle Cyril,
de-mobbed from the Navy, and me, at eight.
I stare at the breakers: horses' manes
tossed in cavalries of galloping spray.
"The sea always remembers our past,"
he whispered. I try again: long curved
lines of choirboys with tumbling white
surplices, singing in high voices of salt.

He pulled his cap over his eyes again.
Midshipman Cyril had floated off-shore,
covered in oil, after his frigate was bombed.
Alive but unconscious. He remembered nothing
but a tot of rum with shipmates moments before.
For the rest of his life, he tried to avoid
looking at beaches with the tide coming in.
In the roar of the surf, he'd hear a murmuring:
why couldn't they have been saved like him?

Long after his death, and in the same bay,
I stare at a backwash of backpacks,
a plastic surf of unsucked straws,
rippling currents of water bottles...
With no shell to my ear, a murmuring:
why couldn't the sea be saved
as much as us? The tide recalls
perfectly every neap and rip in our lives.
It'll keep on coming, whether it lives or dies.

Dawn Steiner

Paired

when did it start
this predawn waking
this need
to watch
the curved weariness of your body
stretched out beside me
check for signs of movement
lean in and listen
for your breathing

the two of us
intertwined
which one will outlive the other

my mother died six weeks after my father
her arteries clogged with grief

I ask you to turn on your side
let me have me some covers
you want to spoon
I feel your breath on the nape of my neck
and I sleep

East Wing Room3557

it's strange
the way the eye eases
from bedside tray
fruit cups and crackers
to yellow tulips
etched against city lights

a blue vinyl chair
cornered to the window
a tan recliner
sheeted and pillowed
for my brother
the overnight companion
in this room where time
measured in millilitres
drips into a body
growing clusters of tumours
like grapes-
a body betrayed

two hours
before the next Dilaudid

my brother and I speak of possibilities
probabilities.
she will get through this. I say

I want to say *I love you*
but can't
love never a word bandied about in our family

Lee Beavington

Leafless

I drive home to Westwood
the horizon
                is wrong

too bright   too wide   too blue

leafless clouds I should not see

                The Trees

have been taken

forty years we grew together
green seedling to longhair

now sidewalked   subdivided

another neighbour has developed
   a taste for progress

my steady-state universe
tilted perpendicular

the horizon
                is wrong

fir
pine
alder
cedar
stacked
delimbed

maple corpses now cast no shade
their last shadows gifted
to those who cut them down

my neighbour has houses to build
yet each tree is home
to one thousand species
now levelled into sawdust
human need
                   is clear cut

too bright   too wide   too blue

the horizon
               is wrong

to cut an old tree
   is to cut a bridge to heaven
      the ancients remind me
I too am rooted
in fertile darkness

I stretch my human fingers
                     not far enough
only leaf veins
touch the blood of the sun

I pull into the driveway
the sky
        stares
                me
                        down

these trees cannot be fixed
with a price
leaf's currency is measured
   one breath at a time

Elizabeth Greene

Blue Roof Farm Revisited

That house will never let her go, says Helen.
It hasn't. Kim, 89, bent, silvery, warm brown eyes,
light starting to fall through her, leads us
to her long low kitchen, wood floors scuffed from
generations of children and dalmatians
(gone now, the house marking their absence
with silence).   The large south window
frames a perfect picture: towering English walnut,
pond, waterfall, red canoe drawn up on land for winter,
November bleached stalks and grasses,
gardens overgrown, but with the bones of care.
Close by, jays, bluer than elsewhere,
masked chickadees dip to the feeder. Chipmunks,
red-tailed squirrels dart along the lawn,
disappear behind stalks of dry spent phlox.
In winter, deer will crowd round the walnut base,
grateful for the food Kim's poured for them.

Outside, if you know where to look,
you'll find Al Purdy's weeping elm,
Roy Kiyooka's golden willow,
bpNichol's sumacs,
Bronwen's lilacs.

Inside, I miss Kim's paintings of factories in winter,
of northern hills and brush. They've sold, settled
into museums or grander rooms
as if they'd always been there.
One enormous oak (not Kim's) remains,
spread over the back wall.
Further back, small photographs of water drops and ice,
soft-eyed does, snow on their noses,
bring the outside to an inner hall.

Things are different now, says Kim.
The weather's different. Something's ending.
Or beginning. I can't tell which.
I'm glad for the young people—
it will give them chances.

In age, Blue Roof, its work not done,
drowses and waits.

Previously published in, Juniper, and in League of Canadian Poets, Poetry Pause, 2018; forthcoming in, No Ordinary Days (Inanna, 2023).

Ellen S. Jaffe

Moving – New York City, 1954

When I was nine, we moved from Central Park West to Park Avenue – not so far away in distance, a world away in attitude.

"The neighbourhood is going down," my parents said about our west-side neighbourhood – even my parents, who'd voted for Adlai Stevenson, opposed Joe McCarthy, cheered for Jackie Robinson, and cried when the Rosenbergs were executed.

They meant the Puerto Ricans, but no one said that out loud. And my Aunt Betty talked about the "*Schvartzes*" (Blacks, then called Negroes) – even at nine, I knew Jews shouldn't be prejudiced toward other people, we'd been victims ourselves. Anyway, it was just wrong.
But what could I do, being only nine?

On Park Avenue, we lived in an apartment building like a fortified castle, six stone buildings around a central courtyard. There were elevator men and doormen (all men).

No one ever took me to Rivington Street on the Lower East Side, where my great-great-grandparents had lived and run their butcher shop. I learned their address, 172 Rivington, years later, going through my mother's photograph album and finding an invitation to my great-grandmother Mary's wedding, 1890, and a wedding photograph of the couple. The lady in the picture was not the great-grandmother I knew, with her wide lap, her apple cake, geraniums on her window-sill. I never knew her husband, Wolf; he died when my mother was five.

I go see the tenement building, still standing though the butcher store is gone. I imagine my great-grandmother looking out the window, above the iron fire escapes. I bring my son, to see ghosts of people he never knew.

After we moved, I went to the same elementary school, but my friends still lived on the upper West Side. The divide kept getting harder to cross.

A longer version of this piece was published in, The Day I Saw Willie Mays and Other Poems, Ellen S. Jaffe. Pinking Shears Publications, Hamilton, 2019.

Richard Harrison

Water Birth
– for Keeghan

With neither language nor a cry, you made me your father
The day you were born in a kiddie pool in our living room, and
You slid, calm as silver, beneath the surface of the water.

And they were green the way green trees bend toward the river,
Your mother, sister, the women around us crying out, reaching, as
With neither language nor a cry, you made me your father.

If I revere you here, it is a warning against my size, so revere
You I will: I whispered, *Like a god* of your face that flattened moment
You slid, calm as silver, beneath the surface of the water.

Then you did not know what you did *not* breathe was air,
For you were made full in a place without questions.
With neither language nor a cry, you made me your father.

And when they lay your blood across my scissors,
I swung the hinge on the door between your last life and this where
You slid, calm as silver, beneath the surface of the water.

You sit under the wind of this dry country like a settler,
in a chair made just your size in the room where you were born.
With neither language nor a cry, you made me your father.
You slid, calm as silver, beneath the surface of the water.

Previously published in, Worthy of His Fall, Wolsak & Wynn, 2005.

Birth Day: The Video
– *for Emma*

The space of writing does not open like a door even though it is the eve of your first birthday and the windows of our city shimmer tonight like candles waiting for the big breath of a wish. We videoed your birth, your mother and her midwives and I together in the bedroom of our house; we thought of our first present to you as the address of your birthplace, the familiarity of your first bed. You were stuck in transition for a long time. I tell you this not to exact a price but because of the way my eyes were opened on your mother that day; away from where she groaned in the bedroom we took ourselves aside and discussed a C-Section, the trip to the hospital unless or if. I admired her also the way I admire athletes, exerting herself for a purpose – we used this language to prepare ourselves – those groans were the groans of a woman who did not allow the body to stop her. But I find it hard, almost impossible, to watch the video now; it unshields me in a way I did not think it would, in a way being there, holding her, then you, did not. When I say I will write this, she tells me, Remember how she was born because they lost the sound of her heart, why I had to push so hard and fast, tearing skin because of that silence. May this always be a gift we give; we could not wait to hear you.

Previously published in, Big Breath of a Wish, Wolsak & Wynn, 1998

When We Were Very and I Was Young

Now I remember my mother's voice:

> *James, James,*
> *Morrison Morrison*
> *Weatherby George Dupree*

    before I knew anything. It's her reading Milne
to my brother and me just after he was born,
    so I was only three and all of memory a tone.

Words come later, then move backwards in time
    and fill in the space where the human voice
        is comforting and untranslatable as birdsong.

I'm 63, and I took great care of my mother,
    yet still, she disappeared at the end of town
        without consulting me.

Growing up is shutting out childhood.
    Growing old is letting it back in.

I recall my mother's voice.
    There was a time before her torments,
    even after they had long dug in.

        There was a time together
when we were very and I was young.

Glenn Kletke

Reclamation

a cold accompaniment
I took for granted

you that I misplaced
without a second thought

so many decades ago
I cannot count them

your onion domes
your empty elm streets

your heart so well hidden
no one ever found it

my little outstretched city
in the middle of nowhere

Guy Simser

Sounds of September 1939

Last week, he thought he had heard everything: his first bell-clanging streetcar ride from Mimico to the CNE fairgrounds to watch dogfighting biplanes roar up into sputtering overhead loops, then lemon-yellow stock cars growling up dirt-track ramps to fly through flaming hoops; and motorcycles farting up around, up around inside a giant wooden barrel, all the way to his hand covered ears and eyebolt eyes.

Today, with warm sun above and fresh lake breeze fanning his hand-clipped blonde hair, he sits in village front lawn tranquility, short-pant hip warm against mom's hopsacking dress. They're sipping homemade iced lemonade. From nearby copse chickadee and finch birdsong sprinkles the air. Gleefully, he loudly crunches her cucumber sandwiches and then a cold-cellar pickle. She's on to his game, crunches louder.

Out from the kitchen window screen he detects a chip, chip, chip. Dad's back at the ice-box. The chipping stops with a shout through the window screen, "Dear, c'mere quick, the PM's declared war!" Pickle in fingers she scurries up the scuffed green porch steps. Puzzled, he trails. They place him between them on the chesterfield; await the next radio bulletin. He listens to a weird voice singing, *"Ink-a-dink, inka dink-a-doo...* he turns to mom, mimics it and smiles.

On the mantle
Big Ben chimes on and on
will it ever end?

Mckenzie King, Declaration of War Sep 10, 1939

In the village, they say

his Pennsylvania Deutsch dad tagged the boy *Hans*, and the kid hated it:
that the Archdeacon then admonished the boy, *It is a sin to hate!*
that the boy ran in old rubber boots to stand penance in the run-off creek
that he whispered, *God be with you*, to a creek-side pussy-willow's wink
that he spotted on a cedar branch his carved-soap cardinal fledged by God
that the cardinal locked eyes with him then took flight through the trees
that he prayed to God to fledge his chest too, so he could follow his cardinal
that he felt a deep humming in his knees as if standing beside the church organ
and
that choral music washed over him as he murmured, *God bless the choirboys!*
that the creek cradled him into the holy of holies where he his legs shrank, his nose blushed, chest flushed and his shuddering arms caught a hallowed updraft
that he stole a scary look down, saw flotsam frothing in the roiling creek
that he heard a familiar shout fading away, *Suppertime son! Suppertime son!*
that he spotted his village crossroad and turned to the toll of the Angelus bell
that he circled the belfry to sing, *Cheer, cheer cheer. . . pur-dy, pur-dy, pur-dy!*
then flew off to build a nest in the cedar tree facing a boy's bed room window.

Peeking
out from under
Trusting Creek's shoreline rock
a bone white crayfish's newborn
lamb eyes

Sharon Berg

Sand and Sieve

odd stolen hour
I lay my book on its belly
walk through the dark house
past the children's door
the sound of their breathing
like moths against the light
dangerously frail
no way can I stand
outside their door
the carpet already
under my feet
the baby curls against
the far wall the dark blotch
of the scab and bruise around her eye
a swollen testament
of abuse or accident
(I cannot swear which)
her sister angry and hurt
by one more man gone absent
the reasons never being
reason enough to her
she resents my part
in not keeping him
thinks she punishes me
with half-conscious spite
time after time
the baby wearing bruises
I bend to kiss that face
the black moth that spreads
its wings over her eye
in the thick air of this

breathless sleeping room
she stirs under my touch
her sister responds
across the room
their dreams entwined
and loving the one who harms
as well in her own pain
I kiss her salty ear
and wetly curling swirls
of hair above her brow

this room is filled
with everything I have made
best out of bad choices
the life that grows by accident
or divine intervention
though every father shivers
with news of their conception
no man knows
these children as I know them
and what is lost?
when I rise sleep-starved
the pages on my desk wanting revision
my children receiving only half
my attention a cold breakfast
the chores of the house undone
turning back to those pages
after each interruption I turn
back to my room and reading light
the ink of their dark room
coloured sand in my vial
forgetting the reason
I passed down the hall
my children and my art
a more persuasive call than
hunger or thirst

or the awful hours of doubt
and isolation when one more man
says we demand
the essential energies he saves
for other purposes
for the wilful bitch
of his art
and the bitter nagging is not
my voice never denying
the hard thing it is
to be a provider
when the private dreams
are outside the scope of energy
or sands
when even love and companion
have gone absent
and what there is to be done
is subjugated
by black moths in that sleeping room
the difficult art

Peggy Roffey

"I am born"

our mother, age ten, cried
when she came to the end
of *David Copperfield*
why the tears, asked her mother
I'm finished it's done I miss David
words tearing up her throat
you know, you can open that book up
at the very first page, read it all over again
and there you'll find David, just as before

imagine the dawning on that young face
re-treading a world not lost
re-reading a tale
she thought she'd never forget

eighty years later I remind her
of that memory
open *David Copperfield*
say slowly   *I   am   born*
as she lies in her bed
bleary eyes clinging to mine
like fingertips on cliff edge
scrabbling for mind enough
to recall
who I was   where she was
what was being borne

Ariane Blackman

Holding My Mother

The third time my mother's heart failed her –
in a ward under white, white sheets

I took off my shoes, lay down beside her –
breathed her breath through me

against the grey window, a starling was beating
with my mother's frail wings

This Wooden Spoon

This wooden spoon
old darkened wood

one time a mouse
gnawed at its roundness

nibbling what was left
of a thousand meals

stirred at the stove,
the teeth marks are still there

and the end is blackened
once too close to fire

the handle is gouged
from striking pot edges

my mother's before me –
she stood at her stove

trained me over her shoulder,
her arthritic knuckles

dusted with herbed crumbs
a careful pinch, some patience

she tasted, tasted, stirred –
left *her* marks on me

Richard M. Grove

Fragments of Memories

Mother is living with what is left
of memories, fragments of time
surfing on a milky pool of reality.
It was very cold when skating
with her father, her at twelve
walking when no one else dared
join them at the rink, scattered glimpses
of scarfed faces blurred into focus,
boots almost too cold to put back on,
running home hand in hand with her father.
Now all these years later, knuckles white
gripping wheelchair, running to get warm.
Soft silver hair shadows the recollections
of tobogganing. Was it with her brother
or her children fifty or sixty years ago.

A Rose Bush For Peter

A rose bush was planted today
in brother Peter's name,
hole dug, the best fancy top soil added,
toed in firm with warm memories,
stoically watered.
Memories flooded as I pulled
thorned branches from root bound pot.
Remembrances of farm life with brother Peter,
riding the pigs, screeching, squealing,
tearing around barnyard pens
clenching perky ears, laughing, shrieking,
till we fell from slippery pink arched backs
rolling with hilarity in the joys of brotherhood.

Later we shared girlie magazines, in narrow space
between garages with lustful neighbourhood buddies.
Often we would be on carefree
afternoon bike rides – home at dusk
or hiking the afternoon away with Daniel Boone,
riding creek swells with Tom Sawyer.

Two buds are already formed
on this new memorial rose,
swelling scarlet edges of fragility
courage budding
one for Sylvia, one for Kristi.
They will slowly, ever so slowly unfold,
and bloom into glory as any rose should.

The Sleep
for my father

Sleep dear prince,
now at the leaf-fallen years
of swaying amber grass
you are in preparation
for the timeless slumber,
at the threshold of the great sleep,
the languid undulating endless seashore,
the ocean of no horizons
where sky and water blend
with the mist
where consciousness fades then
vanishes
into the eternal.

Sleep,
sleep once king, of your domain,
now abdicated to stacked boxes of
un-shelved books, time powdered
unworn shoes of a past life,
rows of floor-to-wall-leaning paintings
of a clearer mind
now seeking, yearning for a wall
of permanence.

Katherine L. Gordon

Fragments

The past spilled
onto a shaft of sun
riding sere grasses,
my sister's stiletto steps
my mother's ever-warm laugh,
bright-eyed friends
before the dimming,
fragments in sprinkled sun-dance
in an autumn meadow.
I caught their fragrance
could not keep their shadows,
though they echoed like music
in this quiet woods.

Restless is the Heart of an Exile

This little town holds
a contained and fragile charm
where my elsewhere-birthed spirit
learns to survive.
My sustaining friends candle it into home
though shadows shimmer in curtained corners.
The land of my ancestors, buried in hard-won sacred soil,
calls out to my waiting bones...
I am forbidden to answer,
grieving for my moment to come
when alien soil covers restless remains
and spirit hovers between the world
that barely embraces me
and the pulsing claim of blood and ligament,
heart, spirit and tribal ties
that scream for my absorption
back into fiery particles that stoked my entity.
Wine cannot placate, bread of other fields
seldom satisfies,
a communion I must re-learn.

Glen Sorestad

The Things We Have to Learn

You are a family man, a lifer, have
partnered in the raising of four children,
adults now with their own children.

You believe you know these children
you are quite proud to call your own.
Nothing is ever so certain as it appears.

Death lays a grim hand on the shoulder
of one of your own and you are shaken
to realize how paltry your knowledge.

The nearer the final breath of your child
the more you learn you did not know.
But you believe, too, if this is true of one,

it must also be true of all the others.
You are parents who knew naught.
But you do believe this: despite all

of which you are ignorant, you know
as do they, how much you have loved
each with unhidden and unbidden joy.

Erasing History

Is this not where the farm of our youth stood?
Nothing here but canola field, right to the road.

Where are the fences, the gateway to the farm,
the garden, the rhubarb patch, the caragana hedges?

What happened to the barn Grandfather built of logs?
The sheds, the small wood frame house, the aspens

that sheltered us from bitter northwest winds?
Where have they gone? How can a ten-foot deep

farm dug-out disappear, as if it never existed,
as if it watered no cows, raised no ducks or geese?

A single farm, a thousand stories, grown fainter
and fainter until stories and tellers are lost.

A blooming field of canola, a dazzle of yellow
beneath cyan sky, wind to tally gains or losses.

Poems From the Editor

At my request Don sent me a few of his "family" oriented poems for this "Poems From the Editor" section. This section is a small thank you to Don Gutteridge for his mammoth contribution of reading over 500 poems and winnowing them down to this final 134 pages – a fine collection. It has always been my pleasure to work with Don – a gentleman and a scholar. Over the years I think we have worked on about fourteen books together. It has been my distinct rewarding pleasure each time.

Richard M. Grove (Tai)
Publisher

Into the April Morning

I step out into the April
morning like Adam introducing
himself to Eden, the crocuses
just nudging their pouting
snouts into the everywhere
ambience of the air, and under
a hedge, ferns unfurl
like phallic fans and purple
iris flog their favours
and lilac buds bulge
towards bloom and daffodils,
long enbulbed, break
their maiden in the fertile forge
of the sun. and I feel a poem
poke up pulsing inside,
and my words, April-aged,
find at last a voice,
palpitating on the page.

Legacies

For Anne in loving memory

You come to me in the
dark heart of the night,
when I am dreading the dream
in which you wave goodbye
as if you were going somewhere
else than the domain
of the dead and its aborted bliss,
and we would meet again
in moonlight like lovers
in the honey month, and plumb
the legacies of love and make
each other immortal.

Green World

Spring was in its infancy:
crocuses poked their petalled
snouts into the erogenous air
and tulip bulbs broke
erotic at the seams and nippled
shoots enthused in an incendiary
sun and lactating buds
bruised the bantering breeze –
and I walked out into this
green world like Adam
carrying the genes of Eden,
like Cain proving fratricidal,
like Moses reading the desert
runes, like Homer dreaming
Odysseys, my head bursting
with April words, my bardic
body engroined by poems.

Date

Shirley doing the fan-
dance on Grandfather's lawn,
showing a curve of calf
and an intimate inch of thigh,
twirling her mother's boa
and shaking her garden gate,
as if she were old enough
to be billing and cooing
and we had nerve enough
to ask her for a date.

Bridal

The Widow Bray's feelings
for her blooms bordered on the
libidinous, for she doted on her
daffodils like a hovering lover,
stroked her roses till they ripened,
turned the April earth
over with an amorous hand
and spent her days and hours
ordering this petal
or kissing that one, as bright
as a bride in her flowered
bower.

A Loving Poem

On Honeymoon Bay we pitch
our tent and watch it rise
like a birthday balloon,
and we listen to wavelets purring
along the shoreline,
and marvel at the dew-gilded
grass and shadows breeding
in the dark, and I am stunned
by the star-shine in your eyes,
mirroring the firmament above,
and we are sung to sleep
by the cove's even breathing
and, cocooned, we embrace
our bodies, and I feel no need
to say I love you.

Five for Tom
In loving memory

Going

When I first saw you
in that incubator
taking baby breaths,
your wee fingers still
wizened from the womb, glancing
off any horizon,
I didn't think we'd see you
growing golden into your bones,
but we did, and you grew anew
each loving day
you gave us, and when Death
drew you into its darkness,
we mourned your lonely going,
knowing you would never be old.

A Summer Day

In this recurring dream
you and I walk out
into a June morning,
soothed by sunshine
licking the lavender loveliness
of lilacs, and we agree
that summer is our season,
when everything greens
and plumps, when hatchlings feel
the wind widen under
their wings, and meadowlarks
sing as if song itself
sanctified their belonging,
and squads of starlings blur
the far horizon, and in the grass
between the trees an adder
seethes from side to side,
and you remark that Beauty
is not beholden to the eye
but to the soul that hearkens,
and I do not wish the dream
to darken and find that you
have died.

Baptism

I wish that you had lived
one more day
so that I could've taken you
fishing for a final time
on Cameron's crystalline lake,
where the bass are biting like
barracuda on a binge,
and the afternoon sun
gilds us with luminous light,
and in a far cove, a blue
heron tilts on a solitary
stilt, yellow-billed
mallards manoeuvre smoothly
and loons cruise, and on
this anondyne day
we are blessed baptismal, tinged
with love's wistful wizardry,
while overhead herring
gulls are crying: "Let there
be no more dying."

Dream

Cameron was groomed out of granite
forty thousand years
ago, when Cro-Magnon
and his simian cousins roamed
the combes and valleys of the Earth
and side-stepped the great
glacial glide, giving
birth as it vanished, and these
artesian waters were waiting
just for us on a sun-
thrummed June afternoon,
as if the geological gist
of history held no meaning
for us, for we were here
like those ancient anglers,
patrolling for Pisces on a lake
that seemed like a dream of itself.

All Things

Like all things that love
the light, your soul sang
its own song, fuelled
by its own fire, and you let it
live where desire abides,
and in the unbelonging
of the night, let it brighten
as it died..

Don Gutteridge was born in Sarnia and raised in the nearby village of Point Edward. He taught High School English for seven years, later becoming a Professor in the Faculty of Education at Western University, where he is now Professor Emeritus. He is the author of seventy books: poetry, fiction and scholarly works in literary criticism and pedagogical theory and practice. Don lives in London, Ontario.

To listen to interviews with the author, go to: **http://thereandthen.podbean.com.**

The Warmest Beat,
the Brightest Light
on Both Sides of Life's Tunnel

An Essay on *Hearthbeat* by M.Sc. Miguel Ángel Olivé Iglesias

Fifty-nine world-class poets capture in heart-warming words and fine style what family really means, in this anthological gem *Hearthbeat,* edited by Don Gutteridge.

I have written about the subject in my reviews and essays many times. I have been motivated by the realization that Canadian poets do have an "umbilical" connection with their family roots, understood as a national and historic construct of an individual identity. It tells the poet where they come from and defines them, lighting their path to their futures. The hearth, aptly registered by Webster's dictionary, digital version, as "*home and family life: the joys of hearth and home.*"

Take John B. Lee´s nostalgic poem, "After the Bath," where the poet's reminiscences send us back in time. It is the great poet singing to the great small things marking his early life, outlining his formidable legacy of poems-to-come:

> "... *as my mother*
> *came gripping a towel*
> *a flag of love*
> *she meant for the nation of me*
> *and I newly cloaked like a terrycloth king*
> *a hero of saltwater stripes*
> *ran quickly away from my youth*
> *in primordial mornings kept close to the heel*
> *by the shade*"

The following lines, taken from James Deahl's "Hiorra Summer," speak not only of a poet recalling his boyhood and family attachments but also that poet laying foundation as well as original leitmotifs (landscapes) and motivations to write, which would become a lifetime career:

> "*Every boyhood summer*
> *we'd visit the old home Ulysses built*
> *on the high slopes of Chestnut Ridge.*
> *When thunder invaded the night*
> *I would listen to the mountains,*
> *try to catch their words*
> *when they thought no one could hear*"

I have quoted Deahl explaining his devotion to poetry: "*I decided that I needed poetry in my life… If I could find a way to speak to people…*" Definitely, from boyhood mementoes to a tall poet is what we receive today.

In "Horses Against the Horizon" we read a transfigured Keith Inman: a poet turned into a painter who leaves pictorial, nearly expressionistic, impressions on me:

*"and the children thin
and weak with summer soup spooned
into mouths leaned
over wide white bowls*

*It came sharp
like light cracking the sky
as thunder bent her
into wind-whipped wheat"*

As we move down the book, we glide with poetic proposals constantly inviting us back to the "family womb." Already pictorially provoked by Inman, now we read John Di Leonardo's poems.

Di Leonardo offers his spirituality and aesthetics by exploring and evoking, unveiling and *connecting* in that sentient human drive to build, either with words or with images – or with the overlapping produce resulting from blending both. He writes inspired by images, he turns into poetics *what was already poetry*, as he lets us know opening his book, *Conditions of Desire*, with a quotation from Simonides of Ceos: "*Painting is silent poetry; poetry is painting that speaks.*"

Thus Di Leonardo repaints, in word form, the works of art he so admires. He engages in ingenious labor and materializes a second "reading" – that is, a re-construal of a reality that had been interpreted before by a visual artist – this time with words.

Enjoy these graphic lines from his poem "Sweetheart"
(Inspired by E. Manet's, "A Bar at the Folies–Bergère" 1882.)

"Between storms
your tears like rain,
all colours washed away.

In our bones we all know
sweetheart, real genius
unfurls rainbows in others.

We are deeply moved by Ronnie R. Brown's "Home Again." A delicately penned piece – the poet's eye-heart-hand nexus crafting a highly responsive poem of remembrance and homesickness – that endears our recollections and evokes sweet reflection:

"You pull into that familiar drive
expecting everything to be
the same: crocheted afghan
on the couch, aroma of fresh-baked
cookies in the air, the flowers

A perfect picture and then
they come into view.
Shrunken somehow, their skin
like ancient cellophane,
so slow you hold your breath
as they wrench themselves
from the cradle of easy chairs
to welcome you home again..."

Joyful anticipation from the title and expressiveness of memories are kindled in "Family Album," by Anna Yin. A poet and critic, Anna has all the ingredients to make us tremble with her poetics. Heiresses of a millenary culture of Chinese origin, her veins carry blood of family stock that she holds and moulds in her poetry:

> "They state —
> *my father, a golden lion,*
> *with a kingdom in mind; rolling and roaring —*
> *the darkness descends, with sight lost,*
> *my father, a silent lamb.*
> *They swear —*
> *my mother, a wooden house,*
> *with windows peering through the foggy road.*
> *When too tempted outside,*
> *closing the door and learning to listen —*
> *my mother, a hut for night."*

Our road through so many impressive poetic memoirs I cannot, unfortunately, cover in full in this essay, takes us to Richard Grove's eloquent title, "Fragments of Memories." Because that is what they are, the memories: *fragments* flickering in our minds, which either fade or endure, oftentimes depending on our affective willpower.

The poet puts it vividly, transporting us back in time, telling exactly what it feels like. In between, a mixture of sadness and happiness in recollections melting in the web of time past:

> "Mother is living with what is left
> of memories, fragments of time
> surfing on a milky pool of reality.
> It was very cold when skating
> with her father, her at twelve
> walking when no one else dared
> join them at the rink, scattered glimpses
> of scarfed faces blurred into focus

> *Now all these years later, knuckles white*
> *gripping wheelchair, running to get warm.*
> *Soft silver hair shadows the recollections*
> *of tobogganing. Was it with her brother*
> *or her children fifty or sixty years ago"*

The sad-glad alternation of memory – linked to the notion of old events revisiting, or to irreparable loss – is masterly presented in Grove's "The Sleep," a eulogy to his father. Here the poet blends first-class imagery and innermost feelings epitomized in lines like *"the timeless slumber," "the threshold of the great sleep," "the ocean of no horizons"* and *"where consciousness fades then vanishes into the eternal"*:

> *"Sleep dear prince,*
> *now at the leaf-fallen years*
> *of swaying amber grass*
> *you are in preparation*
> *for the timeless slumber,*
> *at the threshold of the great sleep,*
> *the languid undulating endless seashore,*
> *the ocean of no horizons*
> *where sky and water blend*
> *with the mist*
> *where consciousness fades then*
> *vanishes*
> *into the eternal."*

The editor, Don Gutteridge, at the behest of the publisher, included a section of his family poems at the end of the book. I have then left my comments about his poetry to close this essay.

Don opened his book with a statement, "To the core called family." There is no better introduction to a collection of poetry that celebrates the institution of family in its varied manifestations and ramifications. When we read Don's "Going," our hearts leap out to the grieving soul that writes these beautifully sad lines. However, we seek to find necessary, unavoidable comfort in the closing line…

> *"When I first saw you
> in that incubator
> taking baby breaths,
> your wee fingers still
> wizened from the womb, glancing
> off any horizon,
> I didn't think we'd see you
> growing golden into your bones,
> but we did, and you grew anew
> each loving day
> you gave us, and when Death
> drew you into its darkness,
> we mourned your lonely going,
> knowing you would never be old."*

As a compilation, one of the book's virtues is in the group of poets summoned to make this book come true. Such choice granted from the beginning the literary-sentimental value of what we have in our hands today.

In my *This Shower of Warm Light Upon this Land and Us. Essays and Reviews on Canadian Poetry* (work-in-progress) I quote from a poem by Don, "The Way Home" (from his book *Point Taken*, Hidden Brook Press, 2018): "The way home is thru / the heart, every blood-beat / hums with remembrance."

I stated in my review book that "Gutteridge's *Point Taken* has brought happiness and homesickness to my mind." So has this new Hidden Brook Press release. *Hearthbeat* honors these quotations from cover to cover: family ties and memories beat in the mists of time never to fade because there are poets, editors and publishers who safeguard and remind us, readers, of the worth of family roots.

Where it comes to remembering about life and living, love and loving; we will always have the warmest beat and the brightest light shining on both sides of life's tunnel, the one that leads us into, through and out of existence: family. Poetry certainly eases the passage.

Let me close this review with two of my "family poems." Written for my parents and my grandparents, I feel they fit in and pay tribute, humbly, to the spirit of *Hearthbeat*. You have my word Don was quoted in my two poems long before I read this fine anthology.

Continuity
To my parents
> *... immortalizing the memories. Don Gutteridge*

I have a connection with rocking chairs,
both dad and mom loved their wooden ones
and ended the day comfortably seated before our ancient
black-and-white, light-bulb, two-channel TV set.
Almost fifty years later that image stays with me,
it recurred when I came from school weekends
and entered the cement pathway leading to my door:

I instantly saw my mother smiling from her rocker
a gift of guava pies baking in the oven, black bean soup
boiling in the pressure cooker and ensalada fría reaching
my nose, awakening my taste buds. She knew how I craved
her cooking after a week away from home...

*When I visit my childhood house — not ours any more —
I am blessed again with those visions and memories strong
enough to endure. There are reminders of those years here now*

*with my eighty-four-year-old father who takes toddler steps
out to the patio where his favorite rocking chair, today
a rubber one, awaits for him to sunbathe, and continuity is
safe in seeing my daughters and granddaughter rock their
happiness in their own rockers watching cartoons
in their flat-screen, multi-channel, color TV.*

Poljot

<small>To my paternal grandparents, Enrique and Zeida
And felt my heart hum. Don Gutteridge</small>

*Today I found my old analog watch,
Poljot (Russian for flight),*

*it was in my lowest chest drawer
dusty cracked glass, opaque green hands
missing their journeys around the digits. My heart leapt.*

*It was a gift from my grandparents when I was nine,
you have good grades, they approved with a smile,
we certainly hope it lasts you, they decreed sternly
with their 1970s-grandparent style.*

*I couldn't believe my wrist!
My watch shone in the dark
I'd spend nights smelling the black leather bracelet
looking at its glass cover under my sheets, marveled,
trying to notice the minute hand's
unnoticeable silent movement...*

*My grandparents' demise came long before
my watch stopped for good. I was able to honor
their wish: it stayed with me until
no watchmaker could fix it.*

*That's when I put it in my drawer — till today.
For a second it ticked fond family memories back to me
and this poem took flight from my drawer.*

Thank you, poets. Thank you, Don.

Author Bios:

Lee Beavington is a river walker, forest seeker, and island dweller. He is TEDx speaker, award-winning author, and interdisciplinary instructor at Kwantlen Polytechnic University and Simon Fraser University. His poetry and PhD research explore environmental ethics, place-based learning, and contemplative science education. More about Lee at www.leebeavington.com.

Sharon Berg's latest work includes: *Before the Heart Went Down: Selected Poems* by Robert Billings (poetry and essay, Cyberwit, 2020); *Stars in the Junkyard* (poetry, Cyberwit, 2020); *Naming the Shadows* (stories, Porcupine's Quill, 2019); and *The Name Unspoken*: Wandering Spirit Survival School (cross-genre First Nations history, BPR Press, 2019).

Ariane Blackman is a writer and poet who loves the unexpected. Poetry works include, *No One Sleeps*, LyricalMyrical Press, 2013; *The River Doesn't Stop*, Aeolus House, 2018; a novel, The *Unexpected Journeys of Lawrence Tyrone*, LE Press, 2018. She is co-editor of Juniper, an on-line poetry publication.

William Bonnell's publications include *Moving South*, a book of poetry, and *The Sherlock Holmes Victorian Cookbook*. His poems have also been published in Canadian and UK poetry journals. He was born in Timmins, Ontario and has lived in Hong Kong, Chicago, London England and Toronto. He lives in Cobourg with his wife Clare.

Ronnie R. Brown, lives in Ottawa, Ontario, Canada and is the author of six poetry collections and one prize-winning chapbook. Brown's work has been published in numerous journals and magazines and has received a number of awards including, The Acorn Plantos Peoples' Poetry Award, for her collection, *States of Matter*.

April Bulmer's most recent book of poetry is called *Out of Darkness, Light* (Hidden Brook Press, John B. Lee Signature Series, 2018). It was a finalist in the Next Generation Indie Book Awards in their spirituality category. She received a 2020 Women of Distinction Award from the Cambridge YWCA. April is a poetry editor for *Devour: Art & Lit Canada*.

Lidia Chiarelli is a Charter Member of Immagine&Poesia, the movement founded in Italy in 2007 with Aeronwy Thomas, Dylan Thomas'daughter. She has become an award-winning poet since 2011 (5 Pushcart Prize Nominations (USA). Her writing has been translated into different languages and published worldwide. Lidia is also an installation artist and collagist.

Robert Currie is the author of eight books of poetry, two novels and two collections of short stories. From 2007 through 2010 he served as Saskatchewan Poet Laureate and travelled the province as an ambassador for poetry. His home town is Moose Jaw where he taught for 30 years at Central Collegiate.

Chip Dameron is the author of ten collections of poetry, including his latest, *Mornings with Dobie's Ghost*. A member of the Texas Institute of Letters, he's also been a Dobie Paisano fellow, and he currently serves on the board of the Writers' League of Texas.

James Deahl is the author of twenty-eight literary titles, the three most recent being: *Travelling The Lost Highway*, *Red Haws To Light The Field*, and *To Be With A Woman*. He is the father of Sarah, Simone, and Shona, and grandfather of Rebekah. Deahl lives in Sarnia with his life partner, writer, Norma West Linder

Bernadette Gabay Dyer is a Toronto author, who has published novels, a short story collection, and poetry. She is the author of four novels *Waltzes I have not Forgotten*, *Abductors*, *Chasing the Banyan Wind*, and *Santiago's Purple Skies at Morning's Light*. She is a member of the Writer's Union of Canada and Science Fiction Canada.

Daniela Elza was born and raised between three continents. She immigrated to Canada in 1999. Her poetry collections are, *the weight of dew* (2012), *the book of It* (2011), *milk tooth bane bone* (2013), and, *the broken boat* (2020). *slow erosions* (Collusion Press, 2020) is a collaboration with Arlene Ang.

Kate Marshall Flaherty was shortlisted for Arc's Poem of the Year 2019 and Exile's Gwendolyn MacEwen Poetry Prize 2018. She has six poetry books and guides StillPoint Writing Circles. See her performance poetry to music, or get a spontaneous poem typed up just for you at https://katemarshallflaherty.ca/

Roy Geiger is a former college English teacher, has reviewed fiction and poetry in numerous publications, volunteered on the board of several long-standing reading series, and published short fiction in *Grain* and *The Antigonish Review*.

Katherine L. Gordon is a poet, publisher, judge and reviewer. She has many books, chapbooks, projects with peers. She has a World Poetry Award with some of her work translated to other languages. She believes that poetry is a powerfully unifying force across the globe.

Elizabeth Greene has published three collections of poetry and a novel, *A Season Among Psychics* (Inanna, 2018). Her selection of Adele Wiseman's poetry, *The Dowager Empress*, appeared from Inanna in 2019. Her current poetry collection, *No Ordinary Days*, is scheduled to appear from Inanna in 2023. She lives in Kingston.

Andreas Gripp is the author of various books of poetry, fiction, and visual art. He is presently the editor of *Beliveau Review*. His latest books of poems are *Festival City* and *Selected Poems 2000-2020* (both with Harmonia Press). He lives in Stratford, Ontario, with his wife Carrie and their two cats, Mabel and Mila.

Richard M. Grove (Tai) is the Poet Laureate of Brighton, Ontario. He lives in Presqu'ile Provincial Park where he runs his publishing company Hidden Brook Press – www.HiddenBrookPress.com. At his HBP website you can find a link to his on line Canadian culture magazine called Devour: Art and Lit Canada. He is the author of twenty titles including, Cuba travel memoirs, short stories and a novel, "Some Sort of Normal".

Richard Harrison (home town, Toronto), author of six books of poetry, won a Governor-General's Award for *On Not Losing My Father's Ashes in the Flood* in 2017. Recently retired from Mount Royal University, he writes, edits, and leads workshops in Calgary, where he and his wife Lisa (Regina) raised their two children, Emma and Keeghan.

Farideh Hassanzadeh is an Iranian poet and translator. Her poems have appeared in these anthologies: *Letters to the World*, *After Shocks*, *Tonight, An Anthology of World Love Poetry*, *Universal Oneness*, *Choice Words*. She has translated more than a dozen books, including *The Last Night with Sylvia Plath: Essays on Poetry* and *The Selected Poems of T.S. Eliot*

Rhoda Hassmann has published frequently since 1980 in *Tower Poetry* and other Canadian venues. She won first prize in two chapbooks published by the Ontario Poetry Society (2019), *Open Heart 13* and *The World Around Us*. She also won Honourable Mentions in *The Banister*, 2017 and 2020. She is a scholar of international human rights.

Laurence Hutchman grew up in Toronto. He was a professor of English at the Université de Moncton in Edmundston for 23 years. Hutchman has published 13 books of poetry, co-edited *Coastlines: The Poetry of Atlantic Canada* and edited *In the Writers' Words*. His most recent book is *Swimming Toward the Sun Collected Poems: 1968-2020*.

Debbie Okun Hill is a Canadian poet/blogger with over 440 poems published in Canada, and the US. She has one trade book *Tarnished Trophies* (Black Moss Press, 2014) and four poetry chapbooks. Follow her literary journey on her blog *Kites Without Strings* where for almost seven years she has posted 175 features.

Keith Inman has six books of poetry. His work can be found in major libraries across North America, in Dublin, and Zurich. His latest book, *The Way History Dries*, from Black Moss Press, unfolds like a novel. Canlit compared his previous work, *The War Poems: Screaming at Heaven*, to Atwood, Boyden and Itani. Keith lives in Thorold, Ontario.

Ellen S. Jaffe grew up in New York, studied in England, and moved to Canada in 1979; she now lives in Toronto. She has published 3 poetry collections, a young-adult novel, and a guide to writing, plus work in journals, anthologies, and chapbooks. She received Ontario Arts Council grants for writing and artists-in-education, and other literary awards. www.ellen-s-jaffe.com

Betsy Joseph (Dallas, TX) has poems which have appeared in a number of journals, and her poetry collection, *Only So Many Autumns,* was published by Lamar University Literary Press in 2019. In addition, she and her husband, photographer Bruce Jordan, recently published their book *Benches,* which pairs her haiku with his black and white photography.

Paul Kelley's poems, essays, and translations have appeared in many journals and anthologies in Canada and the U.S. Kelley's poems have been called "perfectly articulated acts of attention... written with the intensity of a last day on earth." He lives in Kingston, Ontario.

Glenn Kletke was born and educated in Winnipeg, Manitoba. He currently lives in Kanata, Ontario. His most recent book is "A Bundled Slew of Dubious Undoings."

Ruth Latta won first and second prizes in the 2017 Canadian Authors' Association (National Capital Branch) poetry competition. Her poems have appeared in many magazines, recently in The Banister; Our Times; Ontario Poetry Society's anthologies, and the Glebe Report Poetry Quarterly. Ruth's latest novel is *Votes, Love and War* (Ottawa, Baico, 2019).

Donna Langevin's fifth poetry collection *Brimming* was published by Piquant Press, 2019. She won second prize in the 2014 GritLIT contest, and first prize in the Banister Competition 2019. Her plays, *The Dinner* and *Bargains in the New World* won first prizes at the Eden Mills Festival, 2014, 2015. *Summer of Saints* will be produced by Act 2, Ryerson University in 2021.

John B. Lee's latest of 75 books include *Darling, may I touch your pinkletink,* and *By & By: poems by Don Gutteridge and John B. Lee,* both from Hidden Brook Press, 2020. He lives in a lake house overlooking Long Point Bay, in Port Dover on the south shore of Lake Erie. Lee is the only Canadian to be a three time simultaneous Poet Laureate: Norfolk County, the city of Brantford, and the CCLA.

John Di Leonardo is a Canadian visual artist/poet and a graduate of McMaster University. He has published two award winning chapbooks *Book of Hours* (2014), and *Starry Nights* (2015). He is the recipient of, The Ted Plantos Memorial Award (2017). His debut collection of ekphrastic poetry, *Conditions of Desire,* was published by Hidden Brook Press, 2018. He writes and paints in Brooklin, Ontario.

Lisa Makarchuk coordinated two Festivals of Poetry of Resistance. Her poetry can be found in *Bottom of the Wine Jar,* anthologies: *Crossing Borders, Things That Matter, Roll Call, Literature for the People, among others.* Her poetry was reviewed in *In a Fragile Moment: a Landscape of Canadian Poetry.*

David Malone lives in Kingston with his family. Several of his poems appeared in the anthology *Not That Forgotten*, also by Hidden Brook Press.

Blaine Marchand's poetry and prose has appeared in magazines across Canada, the US, New Zealand and Pakistan. He has six books of poetry, a chapbook, young adult novel and a work of non-fiction published. These poems are from a full-length manuscript of poems, *Becoming History*. He lives in Ottawa.

Callista Markotich has been a teacher, principal and Superintendent of Education in Eastern Ontario. Retired, she lives in Kingston, Ontario. Her poetry appears in *Prairie Fire, The Nashwaak Review, Riddlefence, The New Quarterly, Wax Poetry, Pilgrimage, Saddlebag Dispatches*, in Canadian and American ezines and in *Room*, where it has received a 2019 poetry award.

Elizabeth McCallister resides in Brantford. Her work has appeared in *The World Around Us* chapbook, *Tamaracks:* Canadian poetry for the 21st century and *Voices Israel* 2018 Poetry Anthology as well as other anthologies.

Susan McMaster is an Ottawa poet, has published 40 books, anthologies, and wordmusic recordings with First Draft, SugarBeat, Geode Music & Poetry, and Solstice. She is a former president of the League of Canadian Poets; and founding editor of *Branching Out*, the first national feminist/arts magazine, and of *Vernissage* magazine for the National Gallery of Canada.

Roger Nash is inaugural Poet Laureate of Sudbury, and a past-President of the League of Canadian Poets. Literary awards include the Canadian Jewish Book Award for Poetry, the PEN/O. Henry Prize Story Award, and being anthologized in *Best Canadian Poetry* (Biblioasis, 2020). His latest collection of poetry is *Climbing a Question* (Quattro Publishing, 2019).

Chris Pannell has published six books of poetry, including *Drive* (winner of the Acorn-Plantos Peoples's Poetry award), *A Nervous City* (winner of the Kerry Schooley Book Award) and *Love, Despite the Ache* released in 2016 and winner of the Poetry Book of the Year from the Hamilton Arts Council.

David Pratt's poetry and short fiction have been published in over 100 journals in the United States, Canada, Britain, and Australia. His op-eds have appeared in national newspapers in Canada and the United States. He is the author of *Apprehensions of van Gogh* (Hidden Brook Press, 2015), _and *Nobel Laureates: The Secret of Their Success* (Branden Books, 2016). He lives in Kingston, Ontario.

Sally Quon spends her time blogging back-country adventures and reading poetry to the cat. She has been published in *Chicken Soup for the Soul – The Forgiveness Fix* and was a finalist for the 2020 Vallum Chapbook Award. She is an Associate Member of the League of Canadian Poets. Her bucket list is entirely about bears.

Kathy Robertson's work has appeared in literary journals and anthologies including *Devour Art and Lit Canada, Adelaide Literary Magazine, Crannóg Literary Journal, Voices Israel, Taj Mahal Review, The Avocet, The Banister, The Ontario Poetry Society, Tower Poetry Society,* as well as *Tamaracks: Canadian Poetry for the 21st Century* by Lummox Press in San Pedro, California.

Peggy Roffey winters in London, Ontario and summers on Manitoulin Island. She posts, for friends, a weekly "Thursday Poem." Brick Books published her chapbook, *From the Medley* and a second chapbook, *The Renga,* a collaborative poem written with David White, Patrick Deane, and Sheila McColm.

Linda Rogers under house arrest is writing and editing her way to Armageddon. Her current project is Mother, the Verb, the Swan Sister Treasure Book, a collection of writing and visual art. She is a past poet Laureate of Victoria, Canadian People's Poet and water troubler. Recent titles include, *Repairing the Hive* and *Yo! Wik'sas* with Chief Rande Cook.

Basudhara Roy teaches English at Karim City College, Jamshedpur, Jharkhand, India. Her areas of academic and creative interest are poetry, women's writing, gender studies and postmodern criticism. As a poet, academic and reviewer, her work has been widely published. Her debut collection of poems, *Moon in my Teacup,* appeared from Writer's Workshop, Kolkata in 2019.

Guy Simser is a former journalist/diplomat, has two books (See c*atkin Press* and *Inkling Press*); won the Carleton University Poetry Prize and Diane Brebner Prize amongst others. His poems have appeared in Vallum, TAR, French Literary Review and anthologies such as, *Journey to the Interior. American Versions of Haibun: A critical review.* Tuttle Co. NY 1998.

K.V. Skene's poetry has appeared in anthologies and journals within Canada, US, UK, Australia, Austria, Ireland. India, Cuba and China. Skene's latest publications include *Unoriginal Sins,* published by erbacce-press (UK) plus a chapbook, *The Love Life of Bus Shelters* in early 2019 from Cinnamon Press. (UK). KV currently resides in Toronto.

Nathalie Sorensen taught English at St. Lawrence College for many years. She is published in literary magazines including *The New Quarterly*, where her poem "On Examining Piranesi's *Carceri*" received third prize in The Nick Blatchford Occasional Verse Contest, (Fall, 2011), and anthologies including '*Scapes Poetry and Company: A Kingston Community Anthology.* (Hidden Brook Press, 2007, Diane Dawber ed).

Glen Sorestad is author of over twenty-five books of poetry. His poems have appeared online and in print in many different countries, as well as being translated into eight languages, including a bilingual Italian/English volume, *Selected Poems from Dancing Birches* (Impremix Graffika, Italy 2020). He was the first Poet Laureate of Saskatchewan 2000-2004 which means that he was the first provincially appointed poet laureate in Canada. He is a Member of the Order of Canada.

Dawn Steiner began writing poetry under the guidance of Stephanie Bolster. As a member of The Wellington Street Poets, she has collaborated on five chapbooks as well as a collection in book form called *Oblique Strokes*. Her poems have appeared in The Voice, Bywords, & In/Words magazine. She is this year's winner of Arc Magazine's Diane Brebner Award .

Brian T. W. Way was born and raised in Prince Edward County (near Belleville, Ontario) and spent his employed life in education at various levels. *Redirection* (poetry), *The Prince of Leroy* (novel), *County Time* (play) have recently been published. His current work *Bee*, an experimental book for all ages, has just been completed.

Max Vandersteen was born in Australia to Dutch immigrant parents who relocated again to Canada when I was young. I grew up in Calgary and settled in Edmonton where I worked as a pipefitter until I retired. I now enjoy the time I have to write poetry and volunteer for charitable and social justice organizations.

Wendy Visser is originally from Brantford, a graduate with an English degree from the University of Guelph and a Cambridge resident who has not travelled far from her roots. An award-winning poet, she is the author of two poetry collections. A good sampling of her work has appeared in journals and anthologies.

Elana Wolff is a Thornhill-based writer of poetry and creative nonfiction, editor, and designer and facilitator of social art courses. Her work has been widely published in Canada and internationally, recently in *Taddle Creek Magazine, The Dalhousie Review, Room, EVENT, Riddle Fence, Eclectica,* and *GRIFFEL*. Her collection, *Swoon* (Guernica Editions, 2020), is the winner of the 2020 Canadian Jewish Literary Award for Poetry.

Jan Wood has over 250 poems, short stories and non-fiction articles printed in a variety of anthologies and magazines. She was Poet Laureate for utmostchristianwriters.com Her book of poetry *Love is not Anonymous* was published by Thistledown Press in 2015.

Anna Yin was Mississauga's Inaugural Poet Laureate (2015-2017) and has authored five collections of poetry. Her poems/translations have appeared at ARC Poetry, New York Times, China Daily, CBC Radio. Anna won the 2005 Ted Plantos Memorial Award, two MARTYs, three grants from OAC and 2013 Professional Achievement Award from CPAC. annapoetry.com

www.ingramcontent.com/pod-product-compliance
Lightning Source LLC
Chambersburg PA
CBHW021445070526
44577CB00002B/266